Peter:
Wishing you continued success.

Sincerely,
Bruce A. Kelly, PhD

The Prodigal Executive

How to Coach Executives

Too Painful to Keep,

Too Valuable to Fire

By: Bruce A. Heller, Ph.D.

AuthorHouse™
1663 Liberty Drive, Suite 200
Bloomington, IN 47403
www.authorhouse.com
Phone: 1-800-839-8640

© *2009 Bruce A. Heller, Ph.D.. All rights reserved.*

No part of this book may be reproduced, stored in a retrieval system, or transmitted by any means without the written permission of the author.

First published by AuthorHouse 7/21/2009

ISBN: 978-1-4389-6026-5 (sc)
ISBN: 978-1-4389-6027-2 (hc)

Printed in the United States of America
Bloomington, Indiana

This book is printed on acid-free paper.

Table of Contents

Acknowledgements ix
Forward xi

1. The Can't Live With Them, Can't Live Without Them Problem 1
   - Too Painful to Stay, Too Valuable to Go 2
   - Why Typical Fixes Fail 3
   - Understanding the Typical Executive Derailment 6
   - They Feel Like Alice in Executive Wonderland 9
   - The Prodigal Executive 11
   - Would You Embrace a Prodigal Executive? 13
   - What's Ahead 14

2. Six Myths That Hold Many Back 17
   - A Tale of Another Prodigal General 19
   - Myth #1: A Leopard Can't Change Its Spots 20
   - Myth #2: You Can't Teach an Old Dog New Tricks 22
   - Myth #3: Once a Jerk, Always A Jerk 24
   - Myth #4: Time Wounds All Heels 26
   - Myth #5: You Can't Make an Omelet without Breaking Eggs 28
   - Myth #6: Cut Your Losses and Move On 29

3. The Prodigal Executive 31
   - Vladimir the Improver 32
   - How to Get Back on Track 34
   - Why Eight of Ten Can Make a Comeback 35
   - Get Thee to Physical Therapy 35

4. When to Hold 'em and When to Fold 'em 37
   - How to Determine If a Derailed Executive Is Coachable 38
   - Determine If Coaching Is the Right Approach 40

- Does the Light Bulb Want to Be Changed? 41
- Why Derailed Executives Reject Coaching 43
- How to Apply the Concept to Your World 46

5. **You Know What Your Problem Is?** 47
   - Don't Be Feedback-Phobic 51
   - Overcoming "The White Binder Syndrome" 52
   - The Family of Origin Dynamics 54
   - A Final Word About Feedback 56

6. **Prescription Before Diagnosis is Malpractice** 57
   - A Crippling Illustration from the Medical World 58
   - Implications for Coaching Derailed Executives 59
   - Coaching Is Urgent; Assessment Is Important 60
   - What is the Narcissistic Leader? 62
   - Next Up, How to Use Assessments 63

7. **The Reinventor's Toolkit** 65
   - How to Plan an Executive Comeback 66
   - Meet Bill, Comeback Executive of the Year 66
   - Begin with the Assessment Stage 68
   - Stage Two Is Coaching 70
   - Stage Three Is Measurement 72

8. **Should I Stay or Should I Go Now?** 75
   - When and How to Help Derailed Executives Out the Door 76
   - Two Ways to Show Them the Door 78
   - Applying This to the Manager Coach 79

9. **Progress is Our Most Important Product** 81
   - How to Conduct "Back on Track" Benchmark Meetings 82
   - Three Success Metric Conversations 84
   - A Closing Plea: Create a Culture That Prevents Derailment 87

10. Career GPS 89
- Guiding Mark to His Goal 90
- All Executives Need Career GPS 91
- Setting Executives Up to Fail 92
- Why Highly Technical Professionals Derail 93
- A Few Closing Thoughts 94

About the Author 99

Acknowledgements

Writing a book is an adventure. For an adventure to be successful, one should not go it alone. This adventure included many people who provided support, encouragement, and at times painful feedback. But without their help, this book would not have become a reality.

I first want to thank my wife Sandra. She has always been an enthusiastic cheerleader about any adventure I want to embark upon. Without her, even the seed of an idea to write the book would not have occurred.

I want to thank my son Charlie and my daughter Elizabeth. For they bring the sense of meaning and pride that has been the fuel for the journey.

To my mother and father who will be able to read this book from heaven.

To Dr. Lois Frankel for her willingness to write the forward and for Dr. Pam Erhardt who has been a colleague and friend.

To Henry Devries for all of his tutelege, quips, and straightforward feedback.

To my long time colleague and friend Dr. Ken Nowack, I thank you for your graciousness and for encouraging me to focus my consulting on executive coaching.

To Dr. John Miller whose friendship and ideas have significantly touched my life.

To Dr. Lori Kleinman who has been a reservoir of encouragement and support.

To Paul LaCombe and my Strategic Growth Forum who provided the tough love to not only start the book but to complete it.

To Claudia Finkel, for being a great friend and constant source of encouragement.

To Dana Borowka, author of "Cracking the Personality Code" for his inspiration and insights.

To Judy Smith, my assistant, who has been a "life saver" by keeping me focused.

Foreword

I once had a boss who repeatedly said, "Managing would be fun if it wasn't for the people." Only after I started my own consulting practice did I learn just how many people would agree with this statement. It began in 1987 with a client, the Director of Organization Development at a Fortune 10 company, who called and asked me to "coach" one of her employees. Keep in mind back then business coaches were virtually unheard of. But I was a hungry new consultant and anxious to hear more.

The client described an executive who was smart, capable, and technically brilliant but didn't have a clue how to get along with other people. When I asked what she had in mind she said, "You're a psychotherapist, you're a trainer, you have years of corporate experience – put them all together and you have a coach." I'm not sure if it was fear of the unknown, naiveté, or just plain ignorance that caused me to suggest it might be better for me to teach the *boss* how to coach the *employee* so that he could apply these skills to other direct reports as well. "Be real," she replied. "You know as well as I do that the boss isn't going to do it."

And with this I became a pioneer in the field of business coaching. With no coaching models to emulate, I developed my own and built a lucrative business doing what managers *should* be doing, but won't.

In the early days, coaching was initially viewed as an embarrassing, remedial process. Meetings typically took place in my office or at an off-site location where colleagues and staff would not be aware that the executive was receiving assistance to become more effective in his or her role. It was a clandestine undertaking. Participation in the process was viewed by some as a "black mark" against an otherwise respectable career.

In a matter of just a few years, however, coaching became a well-accepted, integral part of the many developmental opportunities made available to professionals at all levels of organizations committed to bringing out the best in their human assets. Employees began clamoring for their own coaches and talked openly about their coaching experiences. So much so that companies eventually had to put limitations on who would get coached and which coaches could work with various segments of the employee population. Heaven forbid if the coach who worked with the CEO was also brought in to work with a mid-level manager. Being provided with a company-sponsored coach was a sign that you had arrived and the coach assigned to you was a further signal of your place in corporate hierarchy.

As the use of external coaches reached its peak in the 1990s, everyone from hairdressers to real estate agents decided they could cash in on the coaching craze by becoming coaches of one kind or another. Training programs for these would-be-coaches cropped up around the country, but the coaching model I developed required coaches who worked for me to meet three requirements: (1) possess an advanced degree in a field related to understanding human behavior; (2) have experience working as an employee inside of a company so that they fully comprehend the realities of corporate life; and (3) exhibit strong interpersonal skills that would enable them to build productive coaching relationships. Each year of the last decade of the 20th Century my coaching business grew exponentially and with it the need for seasoned, savvy business coaches. Just about this time I had the good fortune of being introduced to Dr. Bruce Heller.

It was clear from the outset that Bruce met each of my three requirements. He was a psychotherapist, entrepreneur, businessman, and consultant. On top of that, he possessed the emotional intelligence needed to help executives examine their behaviors in a non-threatening, yet challenging environment. As a member of the coaching team at Corporate Coaching International, Bruce was constantly in demand. Word spread through entire organizations that this was a guy you could trust and who would give you good, solid, practical advice to get and keep the job you want. You, the reader of **The Prodigal Executive: How to Coach Executives Too Painful to Keep, Too Valuable to Fire**, are about to become the recipient of the wisdom Bruce gleaned as an executive coach to some of the most powerful people in their respective industries. And just in the nick of time. More and more companies require senior management to engage in coaching while fewer companies are using external coaches to coach anyone except their C-Suite executives. The pendulum has swung and managers are once again expected to develop their people rather than rely on outside consultants to do it for them.

Using real-time examples of people he's helped to avoid or overcome derailment, as well as examples of high profile people who contributed to the demise of their own careers or reputations, Bruce clearly lays out the dynamics of derailment, how to recognize it and what to do about it. He provides you with a blueprint to ensure the long-term success of those people who depend on your guidance for their professional growth. **The Prodigal Executive** is a "coach-the-coach" guide that belongs on the desk of anyone who has direct reports.

Now, if you're thinking that you don't have the time to coach a direct report whose performance is faltering, think again. American corporations are waging a war for talent. The demand for knowledge workers will exceed availability over the next decade. Millions of baby boomers will be retiring. People who derail are most often bright, capable, fast-track men and women with an Achilles Heel that can be mended through coaching. They can't see what they can't see and don't know what they don't know. Chances are someone who reports to you is on the path toward derailment but doesn't have a clue how to get back on track. The high cost of turnover, combined with a dwindling population of knowledge workers, make it critical for you to know how to help solid performers avoid derailment.

The Prodigal Executive doesn't bore you with unnecessary theory, mind-boggling data, or exercises that make you turn yourself inside out like a pretzel. Like homespun wisdom passed down from generation to generation, Dr. Bruce Heller generously shares his insights, best practices, and coaching secrets to help you build the bench strength of your department or business. So put on your coaching cap and add the skills to your repertoire that will make *you* an extraordinary leader.

Lois P. Frankel, Ph.D.

1
The "Can't Live With Them, Can't Live Without Them" Problem

My job is to defuse atomic bombs in the workplace. Not literal weapons of mass destruction, but employees that can blow a company apart.

The emergency send-in-the-bomb-squad phone calls I get from CEOs are complaints about high-paid, successful executives that are causing havoc. The CEOs have no clue what to do and are at their wits' end.

On one hand these executives are former star performers. They had to be stellar to rise to the position they now hold. But currently they are causing problems, big problems.

Some create toxic workplaces that cause good employees to flee. Others are causing customers to complain in ever increasing numbers. The executive's peers have become alienated too. Their fellow executives don't want to speak to this ticking time bomb of a person because they are always abrasive. So they avoid them. This creates a serious lack of communication all over the organization. And for whatever reason, their behavior is deteriorating fast.

So why not just fire them?

Ah, that is the dilemma. These are extremely valuable employees. Some bring in millions of dollars to the corporation. If they go, the revenue goes with them. Others have a specialized skill or body of knowledge. They are the best in business, and there is no way to replace that kind of expertise.

The CEOs are confused because they have tried everything they know to turn these executives around. As a last resort they call me.

Too Painful to Stay, Too Valuable to Go

One hotline call I got was to meet Wayne. Like all names in this book, his name has been changed, but this is a true story. As regional vice president of an international company, Wayne managed several regional mangers and was responsible for thousands of employees. Wayne's role model as an executive was a marine drill instructor barking orders during boot camp. He was known as a loud, intimidating, foul-mouthed bully who could make people feel about two feet tall.

Wayne knew he was a bully and was proud of it. He actually felt the more intimidating he could become, the more productive he would be. Hostile work environment complaints began to mount, and good people began to flee.

"Can you help us?" asked the chief administrative officer when he called in a panic. "We don't want to lose him. He was once well respected, but he can't continue here like this."

So I flew in to see Wayne. As promised, he was crude, rude, and had a nasty attitude. He verbally tested me to see if I was tough. For me, Wayne was not that unusual. For fifteen years I have been busy with Waynes all across corporate America. They scream at me. They heap abuse on me.

They drop the *f*-bomb, the *s*-bomb, and every profanity bomb imaginable. They say things like "Who the hell do you think you are to come in and coach me?"

Good question. I am an executive coach with a doctorate in psychology. Some try to bait me by calling me a company shrink, but I've been called worse. Before my work with corporate clients I helped people overcome drug and alcohol addictions. There is an old adage that says people who need help the most seem to deserve it the least.

Actually, I liked Wayne. He was extremely intelligent and articulate. When I told Wayne my job isn't to terminate people but to help the best to get better, that calmed him down.

"Wayne, why do think I am here?" I asked him.

He replied, "Maybe people find me intimidating."

"No, Wayne, you are intimidating," I told him. "But you are the best at what you do. Tiger Woods only got better when he went to a coach. Whatever you are doing isn't working. It is up to you if you want the coaching your company is willing to pay for. Your only hope to stay here is to work with me to create a new executive brand for you."

Why Typical Fixes Fail

Actually the problem isn't that unusual. Many companies have highly skilled employees or those in a leadership role that are too good to fire and too bad to keep. The impact on turnover can be devastating. Given the fact that 63 percent of employees who do not feel respected in the workplace intend to leave within two years, versus 19 percent of those who feel respected, companies cannot afford to let these situations fester for long (Nowack, 2006, "Coaching Competent Jerks: Can Zebras Change Their Stripes?").

My purpose is to help managers at any level coach their derailed employees back to success. Almost all companies have this issue to some degree and don't know what to do. First, they try to fix it on their own. CEOs tell their human resources (HR) departments to go have a conversation with the person.

So HR meets with the out-of-control executive and relays the complaints they are hearing. They offer to send the executive to an anger management class or take what's called a multi-rater or 360-degree feedback survey. These feedback instruments are designed to enhance and consequently improve managerial behavior (London and Beatty, 1993, "360-degree as a competitive advantage," Human Resource Management).

What is always missing with a class or a 360-degree assessment is lack of accountability. Nobody sits down with the executive, gives them practical action items to work on, and then checks in with them to see how they are progressing. Everyone in an organization is suffering from "time famine" and spends time on the urgent and not the important.

What is needed is someone to hold them accountable for change. The data from the assessment or the workshop exercises gives them a diagnosis, but not the prescription. Without a prescription one can not ever get better.

Weekend workshops can be helpful, but the issue is if there is no follow up the materials go into a white binder never to be used again. Even if they have the best of intentions, on Monday these executives get swamped with phone calls and problems that keep them too, too busy. This has been called the tyranny of the urgent over the important. The executives tell themselves "I will work on it tomorrow." And tomorrow never comes.

When the assessments and the classes don't work, then HR tries something else. They have the troubled executive and his or her manager "talk about the issue" on a regular basis. On the surface, this is the right idea in theory but typically damned to failure in practice.

Can you guess why this doesn't work? Because managers don't like to give feedback and don't know how to give feedback. Giving feedback is a challenge, and their approach is usually based on how they were parented. The meetings are not held on a regular and consistent basis.

Probably the worst phrases in the English language are "we need to talk" and "let me give you some feedback." Nothing good ever comes after those words. Managers want good rapport with the people who work for them, and giving unsolicited bad news is a rapport killer.

So what does work? Coaching.

There is a big difference between feedback and coaching. With coaching you want to know what to do to get better. We all need coaching that helps us learn.

First, consider the different ways you can learn anything. You can learn by experimenting (trial and error), reading a book (I am glad you are reading this one), attending a half-day seminar, attending an all-day workshop, or taking a multi-day course. But the best way to learn is through coaching with a three-step process. First the coach tells you what to do. Second, the coach shows you how to do it through practice sessions. Finally, the coach lets you start doing it but is there to give you direction so you can hone in on success.

Understanding the Typical Executive Derailment

Researchers have found that many of the strengths that lead high-potential managers to early promotions become weaknesses. As they rise through the ranks they eventually fail to make the transitions required to deal with the increasing complexity they face. When that happens, many managers whose careers were on the rise stumble. They derail. In fact, perhaps 30 to 50 percent of high-potential managers and executives derail (Lombardo and Eichinger, 1995, *Preventing Derailment: What to Do Before It's Too Late*).

Over the years I have found the case histories of these "too good to fire, too bad to keep" executives follow a similar pattern. In my opinion these are the worst kinds of executive derailments. Once these executives were on the right track. They were successful and rose through the business world. They felt good about their increasing responsibilities and status. This is the anticipation stage. They and those around them anticipate their career will keep rolling along.

But then things go awry. Something causes them to derail. This is the frustration stage, when what got them to this level of success is not working any more. These people are hard workers, so they are determined to work harder and harder to improve the situation. All this really does is accelerate the problem.

Finally comes the nightmare stage. At this point we are past derailment; we are headed for a full-blown train wreck. Things are approaching the breaking point, and the company feels there is no other way out but to fire them. This is demoralizing for the executive and a great loss for the organization.

That's how it went for Joe. When I was called in to meet Joe I found him to be likable, smart, and articulate. He did creative technical work and was one of the very best at it in his field. Direct reports loved him, and he had built a great team around him. He had a rare gift in being able to analyze problems in a manner that was both broad and deep.

So what was the derailment? His peers described Joe as one of the most negative people they had ever met. On a negative scale of 1 to 10, Joe was a 13. They complained that Joe did not attend meetings. When he did, he wasn't a team player because he constantly complained about management.

Joe, a football player in high school, was a hard worker who had earned a masters degree in engineering. Joe had risen through the ranks at his company, which resulted in more and more people reporting to him (the anticipation stage). But more and more direct reports meant more and more stress (the frustration stage). Joe began to overuse his strength, the ability to analyze a problem, to point out problems everywhere. The president of the company and the vice president of operations tried to talk to him about his negativity for two years, but Joe didn't see it as a problem.

Then came the nightmare stage. The situation came to a head when two key executives in the company threatened to resign if Joe stayed. Their departure would be disastrous for the company, but the president and the operations VP felt they needed Joe's expertise too. As a last resort, I was called in to give Joe one last chance.

Understandably, Joe was skeptical of working with a coach. He had a blind spot. He was unaware that the intent of his comments were received by others quite differently. He intended to be motivating, but the impact was actually demoralizing.

"In the twenty minutes we have talked you have done nothing but bad-mouth the company," I told Joe. "Let's negotiate a severance package and get you out of here."

To my surprise, Joe didn't want to go. "What are my options?" he asked.

"You need to rebrand yourself, that is your only hope of staying," I told him. "Joe, this isn't going to be a quick fix. You need to apologize for past behavior. You need to change your behavior and be consistent. You are going to be put under a microscope for a long time to see if you really have changed."

"Let me think about it," he said in a low voice.

Joe opted to work with me on a weekly basis. My deal with his president was that every ninety days we would evaluate the coaching, in case Joe was misleading me and not serious about changing.

To his credit Joe put as much energy into his rebranding as he did everything else. First he took all his peers to a one-on-one lunch to apologize for his behavior. He asked his peers how he could help them personally and professionally reach their goals. Joe checked in with his peers every six weeks to talk about their goals. He immediately started showing up for every meeting and was supportive and positive.

Initially his peers rated him extremely low in the 360 surveys, but in six months they rated him much higher. The two key executives didn't resign, and Joe didn't have to be fired. Best of all, the improved situation gave the president and operations VP more time to deal with the strategic issues of the business and not on this personnel matter.

Joe was back on track. He stayed for another three years, then decided to go out on own. Instead of a hostile departure, the relationship he forged with the company that he departed was mutually beneficial. Joe is proof that derailment stories can have a happy ending.

They Feel Like Alice in Executive Wonderland

Before we go further, let's examine this from the vantage of the derailed executive. They feel like a character in a book or movie that is transported to some strange world. In literature these are labeled voyage and return stories. Three familiar examples are *The Wizard of Oz*, *Goldilocks and the Three Bears*, and *Alice in Wonderland*. The plot of these stories revolves around someone who finds themselves in an unfamiliar world and tries to find a way home.

Here is the formula for a typical voyage and return story:

1. Anticipation stage and fall into other world (Dorothy's home plops down in Oz)
2. Initial fascination or dream stage (off to see the Wizard and gaining new friends)
3. Frustration stage (Wizard won't help unless Dorothy brings back Wicked Witch's broom)
4. Nightmare stage (trapped in castle of Wicked Witch)
5. Thrilling escape and return (rescue from castle, clicking ruby slippers to go home to Kansas)

These stories can happen in modern day settings too. Movies about ordinary people getting caught up with con artists, like *House of Games*, *The Spanish Prisoner*, or *The Freshmen*, also fall in this category. Voyage and return can be futuristic thrillers like H. G. Wells' *The Time Machine* or period piece comedies like the Jane Austen send-up *Cold Comfort Farm*.

This brings me to the story of Peter, someone who felt like he was a character caught up in one of these voyage and return stories.

The Prodigal Executive

Peter worked for a company that made large industrial machinery. He was bright, articulate, and charismatic and had tens of thousands of people reporting to him. Through lots and lots of hard work he had risen to lofty, executive heights. But somehow he was dining with me in a fancy restaurant being told that if it didn't work out with me, he was gone.

Why had the CEO of this huge international enterprise ordered Peter, one of his division presidents, to meet with me?

The 360 interviews of peers and direct reports all said the same thing. Peter was an absolute bully notorious for rolling over people like a tank. He was a 6-foot-2-inch, 230-pound bruiser of a man who regularly called people idiot and worse. He freely used foul street language including the seven swear words you can't say on television. The company loved the results, but hated the carnage that went with it.

Peter did make the voyage back to the good graces of they company. He went from his CEO wondering if he should be terminated to still being at the company and thriving five years later.

So how did he do it? As gruff and arrogant as Peter was, he had a sense of humility and appreciated the honest feedback. He thought only results and hard work mattered. He didn't realize he failed to delegate well and the division presidents who worked for him constantly felt like he was giving them a slap in the face.

He was surprised and wanted to change. I informed Peter he had to go apologize to his direct reports. He needed to meet with them one-on-one to be more supportive, more of a resource. "If you miss these meetings they will think you are not serious about change."

Peter was serious about change and took the necessary steps to get back on track. He won, his peers and direct reports won, and the company won too.

The Prodigal Executive

One of the classic voyage and return stories is The Prodigal Son tale from the Bible. Whatever your religious beliefs, there is a lesson to be learned for the workplace from the New Testament parable told by Jesus about a fortune-squandering son who repented and was welcomed back warmly on his homecoming.

The story from the Gospel According to Luke goes like this. There was a man who had two sons. The younger one said to his father, "Father, give me my share of the estate." So he divided his property between them. Not long after that, the younger son got together all he had, set off for a distant country and there squandered his wealth in wild living.

After he had spent everything, there was a severe famine in that whole country, and he began to be in need. So he went and hired himself out to a citizen of that country, who sent him to his fields to feed pigs. He longed to fill his stomach with the pods that the pigs were eating, but no one gave him anything. When he came to his senses, he said, "How many of my father's hired men have food to spare, and here I am starving to death! I will set out and go back to my father and say to him: Father, I have sinned against heaven and against you. I am no longer worthy to be called your son; make me like one of your hired men." So he got up and went to his father.

But while he was still a long way off, his father saw him and was filled with compassion for him; he ran to his son, threw his arms around him, and kissed him. The son said to him, "Father, I have sinned against heaven and against you. I am no longer worthy to be called your son."

But the father said to his servants, "Quick! Bring the best robe and put it on him. Put a ring on his finger and sandals on his feet. Bring the fattened calf and kill it. Let's have a feast and celebrate. For this son of mine was dead and is alive again; he was lost and is found." So they began to celebrate. Meanwhile, the older son was in the field. When he came near the house, he heard music and dancing. So he called one of the servants and asked him what was going on. "Your brother has come home," he replied, "and your father has killed the fattened calf because he has him back safe and sound."

The older brother became angry and refused to go in. So his father went out and pleaded with him. But he answered his father, "Look! All these years I've been slaving for you and never disobeyed your orders. Yet you never gave me even a young goat so I could celebrate with my friends. But when this son of yours who has squandered your property with prostitutes comes home, you kill the fattened calf for him!"

"My son," the father said, "you are always with me, and everything I have is yours. But we had to celebrate and be glad, because this brother of yours was dead and is alive again; he was lost and is found." (Luke 15:11–32)

But what about the end of the story? The older son makes no response to the father. The father wished that the two brothers would embrace and enter with joy into the celebration. This parable, like most of Jesus' parables, uses the Hebrew poetic style, but the end is missing—on purpose. The last missing section is to be written by the listeners who have been drawn into the parable. How would you complete this story? If you were the older brother, would you embrace the prodigal son?

Would You Embrace a Prodigal Executive?

Let me introduce you to Mary.

One day I got a call to meet with an executive at a technology firm that was going into a brand new area. Mary, a passionate and energetic Ph.D., was to lead the charge into this new product area, and she was certainly willing to lead. Unfortunately her boss and peers were at a breaking point because during meetings she would get overly emotional, negative, and combative. Instead of working collaboratively, she just got angry if people didn't do it her way. She would constantly interrupt her peers and publicly criticize them if things were not handled to her exacting specifications. She was alienating everybody at the company.

After initial skepticism, Mary worked with me on rebranding herself. Analytical engineering people like Mary don't like office politics. But a company or organization is political by nature. You need to be likable and make deposits in your goodwill bank account.

Mary's blind spot was that her passion was being misinterpreted as personal attacks. She thought her demeanor was professional; others saw it as aloof. First she apologized to her peers and began to build bridges instead of walls. With coaching, Mary began to curb her tongue. She worked on networking within the company, meeting with people from other departments to find out what they did, how they did it, and how she could be of help. She also worked on external networking. Her political capital with the company soared when she joined some key professional organizations and had an article published in a reputable national journal.

How forgiving were Mary's coworkers? Let's look at peers, bosses, and direct reports.

Peers are forgiving if you are humble enough to apologize and then are consistent in your new behavior. Sure, you are going to make mistakes, but if you consistently apply yourself then you will be forgiven. When you regress to old behavior you need to acknowledge it, apologize for it, and then start doing things right again.

Superiors are forgiving as well. When you first make changes, bosses are going to be skeptical. However bosses, will forgive because they want you getting results. It is why you were "too good to fire" in the first place. They need you to do well so they look good to their boss (everybody has a boss, be it the board of directors or stock price or bottom line).

The group that is the most recalcitrant to forgive are direct reports. A direct report holds you to a higher standard. Once wounded and hurt, they hold on to that for a considerable period of time. But with consistent behavior, they can be won over too.

What's Ahead

This book explains the essentials of what managers and business owners need to know about fixing employees too valuable to fire but too painful to keep on the payroll. My belief is eight out of ten of these dilemma employees can be saved.

As someone responsible for managing employees, this book will provide you with the basics of coaching a derailed employee.

Chapter 2 is about **Six Myths That Hold Many Back.** In my experience it is not true that once a jerk, always a jerk. People can and do change.

Chapter 3 explains **The Prodigal Executive** and how to get derailed executives back on track (80 percent of the time). Think of them as an injured athlete that needs physical therapy. When they get help, the relationships with spouse and kids improve too.

Chapter 4 covers **When to Hold 'em and When to Fold 'em.** This is how and when to determine if a derailed executive is coachable. Much depends on if the executive wants to change.

You Know What Your Problem Is? is the title of Chapter 5. The chapter looks at how to give feedback to derailed executives. The message is help your employees not to be feedback-phobic.

Chapter 6 is titled **Prescription Before Diagnosis Is Malpractice.** The chapter explores how to diagnose derailed executives and the core psychological underpinnings that cause derailment.

Titled **The Reinventor's Toolkit,** Chapter 7 looks at how to plan an executive comeback. The key is to provide training on pro-social behaviors

Chapter 8 is a discussion of **Should I Stay or Should I Go Now?** This is all about the when and how of helping derailed executives out the door if they really need to go. While this book will help improve your termination process and your ability to effectively manage employees, the information here is of a general nature and not intended as legal advice nor a substitute for getting specific legal advice on your particular situation.

In Chapter 9 we discuss why **Progress Is Our Most Important Product.** The chapter tells managers how to conduct back-on-track benchmark meetings that help the employee make measurable progress.

We end with Chapter 10, which examines the **Career GPS** (Global Positioning System) and how to give ongoing executive coaching feedback. Isn't it great how the dashboard GPS voice doesn't shame you or blame you? We need to do the same.

With that caution in mind, let's turn to the process for coaching the prodigal executive.

2
Six Myths That Hold Many Back

One of the pushbacks I get all of the time from skeptical executives is that people can't really change. They just don't believe an individual can change their personality, especially if the person has been that way for a long time.

I say bunk. True, everyone knows that personality is resistant to change. However my experience in dealing with difficult executives is that personality is malleable if there is a reward for changing. They can manage the personality they are given if there is a good reason.

Some executive derailments and difficult personalities get written up in the history books. Consider for a moment the stories of two United States Army generals, both derailed executives too valuable to let go but too painful to keep.

General Douglas MacArthur was commander of Allied Forces in the Southwest Pacific during World War II, commander of the Allied Forces during the occupation of Japan, and commander of United Nations (U.N.) forces during the first nine months of the Korean War. A West Point graduate, historians say he spent his entire life in the Army. MacArthur was born in 1880, the son of Arthur MacArthur, who had been awarded the Medal of Honor during the Civil War. When Arthur MacArthur retired in 1906 he was the senior ranking officer in the U.S. Army.

When the armies of North Korea attacked South Korea in 1950, General Douglas MacArthur was named to direct U.N. Forces in the defense of South Korea. With only the few and poorly trained troops that were then stationed in Japan at his disposal, his forces were pushed down the Korean peninsula. But MacArthur directed a surprise amphibious landing behind enemy lines. His plan succeeded famously, and U.N. troops pushed the enemy north, actually reaching the Yalu River marking the border between China and Korea by late October.

In response, troops of the Chinese People's Liberation Army quietly crossed the Yalu River, struck hard, and routed the UN forces, forcing them on a long retreat. MacArthur repeatedly requested authorization to strike Chinese bases inside China. President Harry Truman was concerned that such actions would draw the Soviet Union into the conflict and risk nuclear war.

In April 1951, MacArthur's disregard of his commander-in-chief led to a crisis. The general sent a letter to Representative Joe Martin (R-Massachusetts), the House Minority Leader, disagreeing with President Truman's policy of limiting the Korean War to avoid a larger war with China. His letters and statements were seen by Truman as a violation of the American constitutional principle that military commanders are subordinate to civilian leadership. Truman decided MacArthur was insubordinate and relieved him of command, leading to a storm of controversy.

MacArthur said "Old soldiers never die, they just fade away." And so he did. This is how his derailed executive story ended.

A Tale of Another Prodigal General

Now consider General George S. Patton III, one of the most colorful American military leaders of World War II, who is regarded as one of the most successful United States field commanders of any war. The general was the focus of the epic 1970 Academy Award-winning movie *Patton*, with the title role played by George C. Scott in a brilliant, profane, Academy Award–winning performance.

Patton's derailment was the notorious "slapping incident" in 1943 that nearly ended his career. According to witnesses and as portrayed in the film, the general was visiting patients at a military hospital in Sicily, and came upon a twenty-four-year old soldier who was crying. Patton asked, "What's the matter with you?" and the weeping soldier replied, "It's my nerves, I guess. I can't stand shelling." Patton thereupon burst into a rage and with much cursing called the soldier a coward, ordering him back to the front. As a crowd gathered, Patton then struck the young soldier in the rear of the head with the back of his hand.

Actually Patton had a pattern of reckless, abusive behavior, and this was not the first slapping occurrence. He was too good to fire, too bad to keep.

His superior, General Dwight Eisenhower, thought of sending Patton home in disgrace, as many newspapers demanded. However Eisenhower decided to keep Patton, but on several conditions. First he must eat humble pie and deliver a public apology. Furthermore Patton would be without a major command. This was a trick to mislead the Germans as to where the next attack would be, since they assumed Patton would lead the assault because he was the general they feared the most.

Why did the Patton's prodigal story have a different outcome? Patton responded to the need to change. First, he gave his apology to the slapped soldier, the medical personnel, and the thousands of soldiers under his command. Next, he redeemed himself with the decoy assignment. Instead of balking at the demotion, Patton was supportive of Eisenhower's and the allies' goals. Patton decided if he was to be a decoy, he was going to be the best expletive deleted decoy in the history of war.

In the months before the June 1944 D-Day invasion of Normandy, Patton gave public talks as commander of the fictional First U.S. Army Group, which was supposedly intending to invade France by way of Calais. The Germans misallocated their forces as a result, and were slow to respond to the actual landings at Normandy.

Following the Normandy invasion, Eisenhower gave Patton another chance. Patton was placed in command of the U.S. Third Army and used Germany's own blitzkrieg tactics against them to hasten the Allied victory and secure his place in military history.

Eisenhower did not accept the myths that people cannot change

Of course, it is unlikely you will be in a position to hire and fire generals. But you do have your own chain of command to look after. With that in mind, let's examine the six most common derailed executives myths in the workplace.

Myth #1: A Leopard Can't Change Its Spots

There is an old adage that says "A leopard can't change its spots," which means we cannot change our innate nature. The saying has been around for thousands of years and is derived from the biblical Book of Jeremiah: "Can the Ethiopian change his skin, or the leopard his spots?"

While there is much truth in that adage, it is not true 100 percent of the time in the workplace. I've found again and again that executives can change their personality, even if they have been that way for a long time. Personality is malleable if there is a reward for being malleable. Like General Patton, they can manage the personality they are given if there is a good reason.

Meet Beverly, an executive with a large financial institution. She was exquisitely ambitious, highly focused, task driven, willing to go the extra mile to make sure everything was done and done correctly. Beverly truly was a star performer in anyone's business model. However, she was seen as unapproachable and devoid of any emotion by the people around her.

What got her off track was not unusual. When we overuse our strengths, they become a weakness. Beverly was so task-oriented she forgot to take care of the people around her. This caused conflicts with her direct reports and a noticeable drop in their productivity. She wasn't making a personal connection with her business connections.

When it comes to improving and maintaining our relationships with others, Stephen Covey's metaphor of the emotional bank account is probably one of the most helpful ideas ever created for developing personal relationships at work (Covey, *Seven Habits of Highly Effective People*, 1989).

Covey says anyone with whom we have a relationship with, whether it be our coworkers, family, or friends, we maintain a personal "emotional" bank account. This account begins with a zero balance. And just as with any bank account, you need to make deposits before you can make withdrawals. Deposits are things like sincere compliments and personal interest in the other person's goals. When you ask direct reports to work late or do extra work, that is a withdrawal. If you haven't made the deposits beforehand, then you have nothing to withdraw, and the account becomes overdrawn. As a general rule, the formula is you need to make five deposits for every withdrawal. Because Beverly was not doing this, her direct reports greatly resented her.

Sometimes all that is needed to change is new information. With coaching Beverly was able to show more interest in people. She now views the people equation as another part of her job, a necessary component to get the job done.

Myth # 2: You Can't Teach an Old Dog New Tricks

The proverb "you can't teach an old dog new tricks" explains why people who have long been used to doing things in a particular way will not abandon their habits. This expression is often used in the workplace to describe how difficult it is for someone who has been doing something one way for a long time to learn how to do it a new way.

There is some scientific backing to this concept about an older person's inability or lack of desire to learn about new and modern things.

A protein normally associated with the immune system could hold a clue to one of the great puzzles of neuroscience: why you can't teach old dogs new tricks. A Harvard Medical School study, published in the journal *Science*, could even create hope for people suffering spinal cord injuries and brain damage.

Plasticity in the brain is its ability to rewire internal connections as a result of experience. Normally this plasticity is largely restricted to critical periods of development early in life, meaning puppies are more receptive to learning tricks.

Now Harvard researchers have shown that adult mice who lack a certain protein have brains that retain the plasticity of much younger mice. Put another way, mice that have that protein are less able to make new connections (*Science*, Aug. 25, 2006, "Learning Induces Long-Term Potentiation in the Hippocampus").

Historically executive incompetence has been conceptualized in terms of a manager not having the characteristics of success (Bray and Howard, *Longitudinal Studies of Adult Psychological Development*, 1983). These included the tricks of being able to delegate, to maintain relationships with peers and direct reports, and to build a team.

However, I believe the notion that executives are set in their ways and unable to learn is just not true. My experience is working with top executives, helping the best of the best to get even better through some season of derailment. I have found that the best want to learn more so they can be the best that they can be.

So how do you teach these old dogs new tricks? You have to do it in small steps so they get success along the way. You also need to help them see how these new skills will help them reach some higher goal they desire.

This reminds me of story of a virtuoso violinist. An interviewer asked him, "What is your number one regret?" He replied, "I should have become the violinist I knew I could have become."

The interviewer said in disbelief, "But you are the maestro of maestros, the best of the best."

What the world-renowned violinist wanted was to be even better. Likewise executives. All top executives are success driven. They are constantly trying to get better at their craft and become all that they can be.

Take Peter, for example. Peter, president of a Fortune 500 subsidiary company, was the most creative genius I have ever met. His level of intuition and ability to analyze problems were superb. He was also one of the best negotiators I have ever seen. Peter picked up subtle nuances and would instantaneously have the perfect retort ready.

With all of those skills it was amazing that the corporate vice president of human resources invited me in to coach Peter.

Peter never listened to anybody who worked for him. He felt because he was the smartest person in the room (no doubt true), listening just wasted time because he already knew what was best. Not surprisingly, there was a mass exodus of top talent from the company.

I coached Peter to listen using small steps. First, I just had him practice not talking for awhile, while his subordinates spoke. Next we had him practice nodding while others spoke. Then, while going through the motions, something amazing happened: he actually heard what they were saying. "I sure learned a lot more listening than when I was talking." For Peter, listening was a whole new trick, and he continued doing it.

Myth #3: Once a Jerk, Always A Jerk

Have you met a competent jerk?

A colleague, Dr. Kenneth Nowack, describes the competent jerk as someone who is difficult to work with or lacks interpersonal skills, but is highly knowledgeable and capable. Sometimes they are "unwavering in their convictions (mostly having to do with them being right) that they are unwilling to take counsel and see absolutely no reason to change their ways" (Envisia Learning White Paper, 2006, "Coaching Competent Jerks: Can Zebras Change Their Stripes?").

Now this is tricky because many executives have been so rewarded for being a jerk throughout their career, being a jerk has exquisite value. The jerk's position is, why change? They see no benefit to be gained from transforming from being a jerk to becoming a decent human being. In fact they have much to lose.

The competent jerk's reluctance to change is understandable. This always reminds me of the story of a very nice man, Bob Newhart, the former accountant who mined his nervous stammer and deadpan demeanor for comedy gold. As a stand-up comedian, Newhart's underplayed delivery and gentle stammering earned him three Grammys and the first comedy album to reach #1 on the Billboard charts. His unique brand of humor translated well to television, where he starred in two of the best-loved sitcoms of the 1970s and 1980s.

When he was doing *The Bob Newhart Show,* one of the producers pulled him aside and said that the shows were running a little long. The producer wondered if Newhart could cut down the time of his speeches by reducing his stammering. "No," Newhart told him. "That stammer bought me a house in Beverly Hills."

For many executives, being a jerk got them where they are today. Actually being a jerk can work under certain circumstances or life cycles of an organization. For instance, this can work well when your company needs someone to take charge in a turnaround situation or crisis mode, but doesn't work so well when you are in growth mode.

The poster child for the competent jerk boss is Al Dunlap, author of *Mean Business: How I Save Bad Companies and Make Good Companies Great* (Dunlap with Bob Andelman, 1997). His tough, tell-it-like-it-is persona stems from humble beginnings in Hoboken, New Jersey. "My parents couldn't afford to send me to college," he says, "so either I got a scholarship, or I wouldn't get an education." A West Point graduate, he believed in screaming at and purposefully humiliating his employees, including top management. Dunlap was so ruthless in downsizing corporations for short-term shareholder profit that he earned nicknames such as "Chainsaw Al" and "Rambo in Pinstripes."

Wall Street loved Dunlap at Scott Paper, where he laid off thousands, but then hated him at Sunbeam, where he himself was finally fired. Another book, *Chainsaw*, by John A. Byrne (2003), dramatically documents the rise and fall of Dunlap, the havoc he wreaked on companies and people's lives, and how he came to power in the first place. Dunlap, unhappy about Byrne's reporting, once said of the *Business Week* writer, "If he were on fire, I wouldn't piss on him." It's a charming quote that Byrne uses to kick off his last chapter.

In my experience, even the competent jerk can change. For me this conjures up images of someone I coached named Stuart, a boss that yelled and screamed purposely to make people feel intellectually inferior. Stuart was leading the company during a turnaround crisis, and he wanted the company to act with urgency. He saw himself like an emergency room physician attending a bleeding trauma patient. In that world there is no time to be nice.

Stuart's management style worked in the short run. But when things turned around at the company, that behavior didn't work any more. If Stuart wanted to continue to lead he needed to learn skills like persuasion and inspiration. When finally confronted with the honest truth ("You either get an executive coach or an outplacement specialist to help you find a new job"), Stuart found the inspiration to change his ways.

Myth #4: Time Wounds All Heels

"Someday this bitter ache will pass, my sweet. Time wounds all heels."

This Groucho Marx line, from the 1940 film *Go West*, is more than the ingenious reversal of the popular cliché "Time heals all wounds."

This is a myth that trips up many companies who have an executive who is too good to fire and too bad to keep.

(By the way, Ann Landers, the most widely syndicated columnist in the world, is also credited with coining this phrase. In 1955, Eppie Lederer was a thirty-seven-year-old, well-to-do housewife and mother who had never published a word when she entered a contest to write an advice column under the pseudonym Ann Landers in the *Chicago Times*. She beat out twenty-seven other entrants, many of them professional journalists, with a column that began "Time wounds all heels" and went on writing for nearly fifty years.)

In the workplace, this misguided belief is that time will work it out. The organizational hope is that the executive will eventually quit causing the pain, suffering, and havoc.

So the leaders do nothing. Typically the board of directors or the CEO doesn't want to confront the pain-in-the-assets executive. This inaction does more harm than good, because silence is reinforcing the executive's negative behavior ("If they aren't saying anything, then what I am doing must be okay," they reason).

Typically I am called in when the company can't wait any longer for time to wound the heel. They feel they have run out of options, and the situation has reached a crisis because of problems like high turnover, customer defections, and even lawsuits for misconduct like sexual harassment and hostile work environment.

Nope, time isn't going to be the answer.

That was the case with Larry, a big guy with a gruff, gruff exterior. Larry was good at alienating people and creating the impression they knew nothing and he knew everything about his area of specialization. Despite repeated warnings from senior executives, Larry was not changing.

In organizations, there are many ways to communicate symbolically. There are ceremonies, awards, logos, icons, contests and oft-told stories. And there are real-life leadership behaviors that "speak" volumes.

My showing up created two pieces of symbolic communications for Larry. One, he didn't believe his job was threatened until an outsider showed up. I was not afraid to confront him and tell him that he was inches away from being shown the door. The other message he got from my presence was the company was willing to make investment in him to be a more effective leader, so he had better pay attention. Happily, in Larry's case, he did pay attention and lost the negativity.

Myth #5: You Can't Make an Omelet without Breaking Eggs

A popular myth is that executive turnover is inevitable—to make a great company, you need to weed out the executive troublemakers, regardless of the value they bring to the company.

There is an old proverb that says you can't make an omelet without breaking a few eggs. This means that in order to achieve something it is inevitable and necessary that something should be destroyed. Some credit *New York Times* Pulitzer-Prize winning reporter Walter Duranty with popularizing the phrase in describing Joseph Stalin's rule in the Soviet Union in the 1930s. For the record, in Russian, the proverb is "when the wood is cut, the chips fly."

So let the chips fly where they may. You can nickname this management style as churn, baby, churn. If the executive derails, then just get rid of them before it turns into a full-blown train wreck.

This just doesn't make economic sense, because companies today must compete to find, develop, and retain top talent. Given the estimates that the costs of replacement of highly skilled workers and those in leadership roles can run up to 200 percent of the employee's salary, the incentive for retaining talent is enormous (Nowack, Envisa Learning White Paper, "Coaching Competent Jerks: Can Zebras Change Their Stripes?" 2006).

Myth #6: Cut Your Losses and Move On

A related myth to the break-a-few eggs approach is the cut-your-losses myth. This myth can best be summed up by the words of W. C. Fields: "If at first you don't succeed, try, try again. Then quit. There's no point in being a damn fool about it."

Yes, some executives need to go no matter how good they are. Many executives when let go actually experience relief. For the individual may be wanting to get fired and as one person said "I set up the firing because of being unhappy and could not pull the trigger myself."

Tim was the director of technology for a company that I was called in to coach. My concern was Tim didn't want to change and therefore wasn't coachable. First things first, I recommend using assessment tools to determine if someone is coachable because I do not want to waste my time and the company's money. The assessments looked fine, but Tim consistently cancelled coaching sessions. He was teeing it up for me to take this to the president so he would be fired. Tim got his wish.

I also took a risk with an executive named Judy. I was the third coach to meet with Judy, and the first two said she was uncoachable. But I was willing to try. After she went through the assessment phase, she began to make progress.

But then things changed between Judy and me. She started to revert to her hostile behavior. She was passive-aggressive about getting information back to me. She refused meetings with me.

For Judy, I was strike three and she was out. Later Judy did admit she was very unhappy in the job and wanted to leave. She just wasn't strong enough to pull the trigger herself.

Not everybody can be saved; you have to be realistic. But in my experience eight out of ten can get back on the right track. Perhaps they won't be perfect, but the value they will bring the organization will far outvalue the pain they cause.

The question is, how do you coach these executives to make the journey and return? That is what we shall examine next.

3
How to Get Derailed Executives Back on Track (80 Percent of the Time)

I have a bone to pick with the late University of Southern California professor Dr. Laurence Peter, the man who coined the term "The Peter Principle."

First introduced in a 1968 book describing the pitfalls of bureaucratic organization, his self-named principle states that "in a hierarchically structured administration, people tend to be promoted up to their level of incompetence."

The book *The Peter Principle* was a best-selling business classic for more than twenty-five years. Why is boredom, bungling, and bad management built into every organization? Through amusing case histories and cartoons, Professor Peter explained how the corporate career track drives executives relentlessly upward -- until they get promoted into jobs they just can't do and wind up driving their colleagues crazy and dragging down productivity and profit.

The principle is based on the observation that when executives prove to be competent in the job to which they are assigned, they get promoted to a higher rank. This process of climbing up the hierarchical ladder can go on indefinitely, until the employee reaches a position where he or she is no longer competent. Typically the same behaviors that helped them rise, wind up hurting them when they reach a certain level.

Funny concept, but not so funny if you are the struggling executive.

During the last fifteen years I've coached almost one thousand examples of The Peter Principle in action. Well over one hundred would fall into the highest category of derailed executive, the worst-case scenario. The good news I have to share is that although their plight is the extreme, my experience is that with proper coaching at least eight out of ten derailed executives can make a comeback.

That's what happened to Vladimir.

Vladimir the Improver

Leadership is such a complex phenomenon in people. Everyone is continually trying to define what it means, but it means different things, for different people, in different circumstances.

I once coached an executive in a manufacturing company named Vladimir (real story, not his real name). He started off as an operations person and became VP of operations, then COO, and eventually president of the company. Here was a confident, smart, and driven individual. Vladimir was very engaging, highly educated. He knew the company and was passionate about it. He had a family that was very important to him.

Yet with all that going for him, he derailed. Vladimir was not equipped to be president. When I was called in, my orders were basically, "He's been a very good operations worker. Turn him into an executive." After a long interview he shared his career goals. He boldly told me he wanted to be CEO one day and that was very important to him. After some assessments we identified that there were three critical areas he needed work on.

When he got promoted he got a brand new office. When I walked in things were still in boxes; nothing was on the walls. When I asked him if he had just moved in, he replied that he had been there for six months. I told him, "If I was a direct report and I walked in here and saw this, my opinion of your credibility would be low. You need to have the office and the accoutrements of the president of a successful corporation. While that may sound superficial, it makes an impression." So he did, even going so far as bringing in one of his basketball trophies, and he started to get feedback that the office looked nicer and was more approachable.

One of his areas we identified, and this is a very common issue, was a lack of delegation. Vladimir was a control freak. He wanted to maintain control because in his old role, the budget was everything. So in his new role he would do things like spend three hours on planning the departmental party.

I sat down with him and told him, "Let's say you make a hundred dollars an hour, and spent three hours on this party. You just spent three hundred dollars. If you asked your assistant to do it for twelve dollars an hour, you only spent thirty-six dollars of labor cost. So you're actually costing the company money by doing low-gain, low-profitability tasks. If you spent the same three hours doing strategic planning, or looking into new acquisitions, that could be worth hundreds of thousands of dollars."

Vladimir made changes that demonstrated he was a leader. Later the board of directors fired the old CEO, and he achieved his goal of becoming the CEO of a publicly traded company. The journey was not an easy one. Vladimir, while he was going through coaching, had both of his parents pass away. So while it sounds like a smooth journey it really wasn't. The eight out of ten derailed executives who can rebound are exquisitely resilient individuals. I'm in awe of them.

How to Get Back on Track

Basically there are two ways to get a derailed executive back on track.

One approach is that a company can internally coach the executive back on track. This involves the HR executive or the CEO sitting down with the executive and providing very clear, crisp, and firm feedback using observational data. He or she gives the individual very clear behavioral expectations and a timeline for them to use and works with the individual to create a plan of action for how the individual is going to turn around every area.

However, the internal approach rarely happens because the HR executive or CEO does not have the coaching skills and background to help create behavioral change.

The second approach is to have a coach from outside the company work with the derailed executive.

My intent is that the insights in this book will help managers improve performance for all of their employees. The purpose of writing this book is to help not only the companies that have derailed executives, but also any derailed employee that wants to get back on track.

Another reason for writing this book is the hope that if executives can learn from what goes wrong with others then they can then look at their own behavior and avoid those patterns. We learn from each other's "failures" more than successes. So if you know what derails an executive, you are going to be better prepared not to engage in that behavior.

Why Eight of Ten Can Make a Comeback

Why can 80 percent of derailed executives make a comeback?

Because these are individuals who are extremely successful. Many of these executives could be compared to an elite athlete. They are highly skilled, talented, and energetic. They have passion for what they do and love the companies they're working for. They feel a sense pride in their work, have an insatiable curiosity, and want to learn more.

Unfortunately, many of them have never had coaching or any sort of leadership development. They were put into a leadership role because they were good at a technical task, and they've always wanted someone to sit down with them and mentor them. As a result, many of them are ripe to learn some of these skills.

There are many parallels between executive coaching and sports coaching, just as there are many parallels between business and sports in general. Executives are similar to elite athletes because they are required to perform at the highest level at all times. Yet, elite athletes train ninety percent of the time and perform ten percent of the time, where executives perform 100 percent of the time.

Get Thee to Physical Therapy

To illustrate my point, let me share the tale of two derailed baseball pitchers that played for the Los Angeles Dodgers, Sandy Koufax and Tommy John.

Sandy Koufax put together one of the most dominating stretches of pitching in baseball history. Over a five-year span, he threw four no-hitters, led the National League in earned run average five times, and compiled a 111–34 record. However, elbow problems forced him to retire at age thirty after the 1966 World Series, one of the saddest days in history for Dodgers fans like me. Inducted in the Hall of Fame in 1972, Koufax became the youngest person ever to receive the honor.

In 1974, Tommy John was having one of his best seasons as a pitcher for the Dodgers with a 13–3 record when a ligament was torn in his pitching arm. John learned from his surgeon, Dr. Frank Jobe, that if he wanted to pitch again he would have to undergo a revolutionary surgical operation that no pitcher had ever undergone.

The operation, widely known today as Tommy John surgery, replaced the ligament in the elbow of his pitching arm with a tendon from his right forearm. The surgery was performed by Dr. Frank Jobe on Sept. 25, 1974. John spent the entire 1975 season recovering from the surgery, and surprised fans and players alike by returning to the Dodgers rotation in 1976. John went on to pitch until 1989 and earned 164 of his 288 victories after his surgery.

"People with a torn ligament were sent back to the farm or wherever they came from," Jobe told *USA Today*. "But Tommy didn't want to go."

According to *The New York Times*, "The surgery has become so reliable, with a success rate of 80 to 85 percent, that it has prolonged the careers of hundreds of major leaguers. About one in seven pitchers in the major leagues this season has had the surgery."

So how does this relate to derailed executives?

The moral of the story is this: We should not think of derailed executives as incompetents. Rather, think of them as star athletes who need to rehab and make a comeback. What is needed is a radical intervention (coaching, not surgery) to rehabilitate the derailed executive. The productivity gains for the company make it well worth the effort.

4
When to Hold 'em and When to Fold 'em

Have you ever had a Joe working for you?

Joe (not his real name) was a big guy, and very, very smart. He was a lawyer who was extremely valuable to the company and exquisitely arrogant. Joe thought he was the smartest one in the room at all times, and probably was right. On top of all that, he was extremely inappropriate with some of the female coworkers. Joe was too valuable to let go and too painful to keep.

Joe was ordered to my office for a company-mandated coaching session. He was extremely angry about that. Joe didn't like the idea of having to speak to somebody else like a consultant or a coach because he always knew more than they did.

"You know what? I'm really not going to change," Joe bellowed at me in the first session. "I don't want to change. I want to keep doing what I'm doing, and I will let the chips fall where they may. And, you know, if I get fired, I get fired."

My response to Joe surprised him. "Congratulations, because at least you are clear about what you want."

The pleasure he got from his inappropriate interactions was stronger than the fear of getting fired. Really, there was nothing an executive coach could do. So for me to continue with Joe really would not make sense. So I just wished him all the best.

Joe wanted to be fired. My opinion is that Joe was so narcissistic, and had such a sense of grandiosity, that he thought the rules didn't apply to him. So he felt that what he did was not inappropriate and didn't see his behavior as harmful to others.

The second possibility is that Joe wasn't happy in his job in the first place. So for him to continue to be inappropriate meant that he was going to lose his job. My guess is that was his underlying motivation.

Finally, Joe was the type that didn't like dealing with authority figures and didn't want anybody to teach him now. In his case, old dogs didn't want to learn new tricks. Joe was not coachable and therefore had to go.

How to Determine If a Derailed Executive Is Coachable

Every poker player knows it doesn't pay to play out every hand to the bitter end. After you ante and see the cards you are dealt, sometimes it is best to fold and minimize your losses.

Ah, but when? Knowing when to walk away from a valuable employee is one of the more complex and controversial areas of my practice because we are dealing with careers, not cards.

The first question that always comes up from a company leader with a derailed executives is, "Can this person change?"

My position with company leaders is always the same: "We never know."

Because we never know what combination of events is going to help this person get motivated. Like the saying goes, don't leave five minutes before the miracle.

Of course, there is always a healthy sense of skepticism that a derailed executive can change. The hiring manager or HR person has attempted many different fixes. Doubtless they have given the derailed executive feedback sessions, sent them to expensive classes, maybe even a 360-degree peer review. All this, and the person still has not changed for an extended period of time.

As one president who has dealt with his share of egomaniac employees cracks, "Let's talk about world peace or something we can *solve*."

The concern from a business standpoint is this: "Why should we invest all this money and time if the person is not going to change. Why take the risk?"

That's always the best place to start. Typically if the company really feels the derailed executive is uncoachable and they've already made the decision that the situation cannot be improved then they don't call me. Instead, the company calls an outplacement consultant to help them fire the executive.

Sometimes the company leader says, "We want to try one more thing before we pull the plug. We don't think the person is coachable, but we are willing to give it at least one more shot."

This is what is called the "get fixed" ultimatum. Either this derailed executive gets fixed, or they get gone.

Determine If Coaching Is the Right Approach

What is the first test for a derailed executive to determine if they can be saved? Whether or not they are willing to go through assessment testing. If they are willing to go through the assessment phase, then the next question becomes: "Is coaching the right program for them?"

There are many ways of determining this. As an executive coach, here are some aspects I consider:

1. Do they understand the feedback they've been given previously?
2. Have they ever had any coaching in the past?
3. Were they in competitive sports, and do they understand the concept of coaching?
4. Are they able to understand that the best get better through coaching and that the best sometimes go through a small derail?
5. How much arrogance do they really have?

If the derailed executive thinks they know everything and can do everything before I even talk to them, then this person is probably not going to get much out of the coaching.

This was the case with Marvin (not his real name). In this situation Marvin didn't see the need for coaching. He would say, "I'm not sure why I'm even being coached. It's unclear to me what the real problem is. I've already made the changes they're looking for. I don't really have any of these issues. I really don't have any reason to even improve on my leadership because I don't want to be promoted."

Obviously Marvin was not a highly motivated person for coaching. In his case the coaching was not the right intervention.

Does the Light Bulb Want to Be Changed?

There's an old joke: How many psychologists does it take to change a light bulb?

The answer is just one, but the light bulb has to want to be changed.

Before you can help a derailed executive you have to determine if they want to change.

The other evidence the person doing the coaching should look for is if the derailed executive makes the initial coaching session very short and really isn't willing to open up and take risks. If this happens, that person is usually a poor candidate for coaching, and I let the company know. That way I don't waste my time or the company's money.

A couple things happen in those first coaching sessions with a derailed executive who is coachable. In most cases the derailed executive tells me they want to be changed. They say things like, "I don't want to be seen as a bully. I don't want to be seen as a negative. I don't want people to think I am a prima donna."

There are three types of responses derailed executives have:

1. The first is the type that acknowledges there is a discrepancy between the view other people have of them and what they have of themselves. These derailed executives put it out there that they do want to become the best leader or executive they can be. They just don't know how to change, what to say, or what to do.
2. While that's the majority, there is a minority percentage who are skeptical because they're scared. These executives have worked

with other people before, and they want to know how working with an executive coach will make any difference.
3. A small fraction of derailed executives are a combination. Sometimes I don't know what I'm going to say until I've tried a few things and see what hits the mark with this group.

A question I sometimes ask during a structured interview is, "At your retirement dinner, what do you want people to say about you? At your funeral, what do you hope the mourners would say?"

Have you ever pondered how your obituary might summarize your life?

Leona Helmsley's obituary said "Queen of Mean, Best Known for Tax Evasion." She ran a $5 billion real estate and hospitality empire. She was listed as one of the five hundred richest people in the world. She donated $25 million to disaster relief funds after 9/11 and Hurricane Katrina. But what she's remembered for is her tax evasion trial and all that came out during the trial about what a mean manager she was to all her employees.

Most people will not get to know what their obituary says before they die. However, there have been some noticeable exceptions.

There's Alfred Nobel, the inventor of dynamite. In 1888, when his brother, Ludvig, died, a French newspaper thought Alfred had passed away and printed an obituary. The headline for his erroneous obituary read "The Merchant of Death is Dead." The article said that Nobel "became rich by finding ways to kill more people faster than ever before." Nobel, upon realizing that this was how the world would remember him, changed his will and gave all his money to set up the Nobel Prizes. He would associate himself with the Peace Prize.

Another person who got to read his obituary before he died was PT Barnum of Barnum and Bailey Circus fame. When he was on his deathbed in 1891, Barnum remarked that he wished he could read his obituary before he died because the press always said nice things about him. So the *New York Evening Sun* obliged and printed his obituary a full month early.

During a coaching session a derailed executive said: "I want my kids to be proud of me." After reporting any negative behavior I would ask, "Would your kids be proud of you if they knew you were doing this?" When the answer was "no" he thought twice about acting in a negative manner. The result was a decrease in those actions that were derailing his career.

Why wait until you die? Get some 360-degree coaching right now. It's going to be difficult to hear, but it will be more difficult for your people to tell you.

Why Derailed Executives Reject Coaching

Some derailed executives say they can't change and reject coaching. But why?

First, let's tackle that word *can't*. To my thinking here's no such thing as "can't." There's either "I won't do it" or "I don't know how to do it."

In my experience as an executive coach, "can't" means the person is afraid and just doesn't know how to change. But even if somebody knows how to change, for them to self-develop and make the change on their own is very difficult. We all need feedback, and we all need support and encouragement. Unless we know what we did and what we need to do and somebody teaches us how to do it, we can't improve.

People don't really self-develop. To illustrate, my son and I went to the USC football practice awhile back and were struck by something at the practice field. At every practice there are four cameras set up on stilts that are recording the action. The players are improving by constantly looking at film afterwards with the coaches. Together they look at what they did in a situation and discuss what they should have done differently. In addition there are also coaches at the practice giving the players ongoing feedback on how to improve. If the team doesn't provide that kind of coaching, players won't know what to change, and they won't be inspired to do it.

USC has won the national championship several times in the last few years. So the question is: "Why are they practicing? They know how to play football." The answer of course is that there is so much at stake they want to rehearse and go over the plays. Likewise, there is so much at stake for these derailed executives. They need to run the plays when it's not in a game situation. Where else can they do that but with a coach who can give them feedback?

For derailed executives there is a useful theory called the Stages of Change Model about the mind/body stages we go through when we do change. The Stages of Change Model was originally developed in the late 1970s by James Prochaska and Carlo DiClemente at the University of Rhode Island when they were studying how smokers were able to give up their habits. According to the model there are a number of steps: precontemplation to contemplation to determination.

The idea behind the change model is that behavior change does not happen in one step. Rather, people tend to progress through different stages on their way to successful change. You first say to yourself, "Well, I don't have a problem. And if I don't have a problem, I don't need a solution." Then you get information feedback and data, such as complaints, and you begin to say, "Maybe there is a problem." So you start to contemplate that there is a problem. If you get even more strong data and a coach comes in, then you have to go from contemplation to determination and decide, "I need to do something about this."

On one hand it is easy to understand why some derailed executives would reject coaching. Many derailed executives don't understand why they should change because the company has promoted them three or four times for being the way they are. Why is someone coming in now and telling them that what got them to that spot is not going to keep them there? Naturally there is a resistance to change an approach that has been so successful for so long. It is a very legitimate concern to wonder why you should take the leap of faith and change. Will this new behavior prove equally successful?

There is a common idea in the business world that you should stick with what works. There are a number of old sayings that reinforce this, from "If it ain't broke, don't fix it," to "Don't change horses midstream."

The reality for executives is that when you rise through the ranks of an organization, you'll find that each individual level has a different set of rules because you have a different function. So what works at a director level is not going to work at a vice president level. The issue is that no one ever sits down and tells you the rules and then tells you how those rules change.

For example, when you're not doing the work, but rather being the strategist to get the work done, the unwritten rules and expectations are different.

To use another sports analogy, when you're in single-A, minor league baseball, the game expectations are one thing. But when you start to get to triple-A or the major leagues, it's a whole different ballgame (pardon the pun). And if you don't make those adjustments, you don't survive.

How to Apply the Concept to Your World

As a manager providing coaching feedback to an employee, you can use the change model of precontemplation to contemplation. As you meet with the employee for a feedback session, be very clear and precise in the information you provide, because the employee is probably in that precontemplation stage where they do not think there is a problem. It's your job as coach to help them go from the precontemplation stage to the contemplation stage, where you demonstrate strongly enough to them that there is a problem.

Also you should communicate you understand that they have been very successful and been promoted because of this behavior in the past. But now because of their new role, this old behavior is not working anymore so they need to change. If you hire an executive coach to do the coaching, then explain that the company wants to make an investment, or give them the gift of coaching so they can have somebody giving them ongoing feedback.

In addition, remember the need and significance of consequence. If the executive that is derailed does not feel that there is a sense of consequence in their behavior continuing, then they're likely not to be as motivated. People are either motivated by greed or by fear, and if they're not afraid that something could truly happen, then there's really no reason for them to change.

If that doesn't motivate them, then sad to say you need to work on their exit strategy. This is the time to lay down your cards and fold.

5
You Know What Your Problem Is?

Pity poor Gunther.

Gunther (real story but not his real name) was told by his manager that he was one of the most negative, rebellious, and insubordinate employees the manager had ever met. If he weren't so technically skilled, he would have been fired long ago.

As I got to know Gunther I realized, and the assessment tools confirmed it, that Gunther was a problem solver, optimistic, and a hard worker. Why the mismatch in opinions? To find out I asked Gunther to run through a recent scenario, and he said:

"Well, my manager asked me to do something, and I started to reflect upon how I was going to solve the problem, and I was talking out loud."

I asked Gunther, "Are you aware that when you're brainstorming out loud how you're going to solve the problem, the perception is that you're giving all the reasons why the project won't work? So your intent is to try to solve the problem, but the impact is that your manager thinks you're being insubordinate. So what I want you to do is next time your manager asks you to take the hill, say 'Yes, boss,' and go into your office and do your problem solving."

Once Gunther began to follow this advice, the difference was amazing. But he was never aware of this problem until it was almost too late, because no manager ever gave him feedback.

Proper feedback can be the difference keeping and losing a valuable employee. According to the U.S. Bureau of Labor Statistics there will be a shortage of more than 10 million workers by 2010 (Herman and Gioia, *Impending Crisis*, 2003). Can you afford to waste even one valuable employee?

Hiring an external coach has been a mainstream approach for management and executive development for many years. In fact, engaging professional coaches to work with managers on their development has become a regular occurrence in most large U.S. corporations. Gone is the stigma of an executive needing a coach to help with development. In fact, a coach can be seen an executive perk.

A newer trend is the emerging role of the internal coach, as managers are "expected to foster the development of their staff as well as to be prime movers of their own growth" (Frish, "The Emerging Role of the Internal Coach," *Consulting Psychology Journal*, Fall 2001).

Before you as a manager get involved in any kind of coaching of a derailed executive, one of the questions you should ask is, "Has this particular executive been given feedback about their behavior?" In my experience, half the time the answer is yes, and half the time, no.

When managers ask me to give them coaching suggestions, there are a few proven concepts that I share on how to give feedback so the employee realizes they're in potential derailment.

Here are my ironclad rules for giving feedback.

Ironclad Rule 1. When you do give feedback, make sure that it is data-based, and behavioral-based. Make sure it is not hearsay. For instance, what is the exact behavior the individual is showing that causes concern? The other day I had a meeting, and this particular executive was given the feedback that it was not acceptable for him to go into a meeting and, when he didn't like an idea, to actually show and express his anger.

Ironclad Rule 2. Always use the sandwich technique. Open with positive feedback, then give the negative feedback, and then close with positive feedback. So there you at least work toward salvaging some of the self-esteem of the individual, by saying: "You're quite a valuable component of our company. You're highly successful, and we want to do everything we can to salvage our relationship. However, we have some concerns, and our concerns are: A, B, C, D, and E."

Then you allow them to give you feedback in return to assess their reaction. Sometimes they're stunned or get angry. One executive, after being given feedback, just got up and left the room without saying a word.

Always end one of these sessions with something positive. Try an approach along the lines of, "We really would like to make an investment with you. As your supervisor, the investment I'm going to make is that I'm going to start spending time with you on a weekly basis. You and I will be putting together a development plan. Whatever resources you need from me or the organization, I'd like to be your champion for the change."

Ironclad Rule 3. Your goal should be to gain some buy-in from the individual. Something like, "Oh, that makes sense" would be the aim.

One of the mistakes supervisors make after giving some coaching feedback is that they don't schedule the next meeting. Before both of you leave after the feedback, say, "Let's you and I meet next Friday morning at 8:30 a.m., and let's continue this conversation."

When you sit down with someone, the first thing you should do is make them feel as comfortable as possible. The second is to do what you can to maintain their self-esteem. The third thing is, when you share your concerns, make sure you:

- don't overwhelm the person with a laundry list
- don't use other people's names, such as, "John said this about you…"
- don't do all the talking

Instead, do really work towards the pattern of behavior you've seen. Give feedback comments such as, "We've seen you get angry in three separate manager meetings by raising your voice, staring someone down, and using inappropriate language."

That makes the derailed executive who is feeling ambivalent go through the precontemplation stage into the contemplation stage. The executive now has enough information to prevent them from going into mental hiding.

When in a coaching session also ask the person about solutions. "Do you have any solutions to the problem that you would like to offer before we get into our solution?" Try to get them to be a partner with you in making a change.

If they say, "Yeah, here are the three things I'd like to do," then you can get it down in writing and put together a plan that you can walk the person through. The plan must cover the behaviors you are trying to change and the behaviors you need the employee to continue or decrease or increase.

Ironclad Rule 4. There needs to be some consequence so the person doesn't just blow off the feedback session. Something you need to do in the first (or second at the latest) coaching session is say, "You know,

Bill, if this behavior doesn't change, then we'll have a discussion about what might be a better fit for you."

So you put the idea of separation out there. They need to know their behavior could lead to termination. If employees don't have a consequence, they don't take the coaching seriously.

One of the cardinal mistakes for the manager is canceling a follow-up meeting. Do not cancel the session. If you have to, make sure you reschedule it for the same day. Here's why. The first time you cancel, the person says, "See, they didn't really believe in this stuff anyway." This is also called symbolic communication. By saying one thing (scheduling a meeting), but then doing another thing (canceling the meeting) you've conveyed that the meeting is not really important.

Don't Be Feedback-Phobic

Of course, it is human nature that people don't want to give other people bad news. That is why there are expressions like, "Don't shoot the messenger." Deep down people want to be seen as likable, the nice guy or gal. Because they want to be nice, giving people negative, but necessary, feedback is the hardest thing for them to do.

The classic example is the senior executive who gave performance appraisals in the restroom. This manager would see the employee in the restroom and hand the person a folder with things they were doing well and not well.

Regardless of the reason, if you are a manager and you don't give somebody in your organization negative feedback, it borders on being unethical. You're carrying information the employee needs to know for their career survival. If that person doesn't succeed but could have if they had the information, then you as their manager have set them up for failure.

The other problem that happens in executive organizations is that the higher up you go, the less feedback you get.

In the words of Dr. Marshall Goldsmith, the author of nineteen books on leadership, "All other things being equal, your people skills (or lack thereof) become more pronounced the higher up you go. In fact, even when things are not equal, your people skills often make the difference in determining how high you go" ("Behave Yourself," *Talent Management Magazine*, July 2007).

Too often, the feedback a high-level executive receives is so sanitized because of politics that it is of scant value. So many times executives, when they do finally get this level of feedback that they're potentially derailing, are very surprised. And some of the comments are, "Well, why wasn't I told this before?" And part of that is the fear of telling the boss there's a problem.

Overcoming "The White Binder Syndrome"

Do you suffer from The White Binder Syndrome?

My first encounter with The White Binder Syndrome came through Marvin, an executive coaching client. Marvin (true story, but not the true name) was one of the smartest people I've ever met. He was a scientist and was energetic, focused, and hard working. When I first walked into his office, he was the VP of a technology company. I asked him how I could help him.

"I really need to become a better leader," Marvin said.

"What have you done previously?" I asked.

So he opened up his cabinet. Inside were eleven white binders from the finest business schools and leadership development programs in the country. At first I was intimidated.

"Well, what do you need me for?" I said, "You've been to some very good and reputable leadership programs."

"I know," he replied. "But nobody has taken all of that data and all these reports and sat down with me and said, 'Here are the steps you need to take to make the improvement.' And no one has ever kept me accountable."

So the White Binder Syndrome is something I see all the time, and that is when a company says, "Oh, just make a beautiful evaluation, and the person will self-develop."

And I say, "No, you won't be happy with my coaching because I'll make a beautiful white binder for you, and it's just going to be put on the shelf."

What's going to happen is the person who gets the feedback says: "Tomorrow I'm going to start self developing."

They wake up in the morning, they put their white binder on the table, and they get their first phone call. The first phone call is the first crisis. So they say to themselves:

"You know, right after lunch I'm going to work on my development."

By the time after lunch comes they already have a list of return phone calls and return e-mails, a separate crisis each. So they say:

"Well, at the end of the day I'm going to work on my development."

At the end of the day, they're tired and they need to go home. This process occurs for about three days until finally they get so frustrated that they put the white binder up on a shelf, never to be seen again.

And that's when The White Binder Syndrome has taken another victim.

The Family of Origin Dynamics

When giving feedback, you need to provide a sense of consequence. People, when they come into an organization, bring their Family of Origin Dynamics into the organizations. The Family of Origin Dynamics is where we learn how to interact with each other, about authority figures, about good/bad consequences, our social skills, and our work ethic.

So when you come into an organization, you come in with these dynamics. In the majority of cases you're not even aware of it. In a few instances one of the executives I'm working with, Al, would go into a meeting and never say anything. He was very smart, and a great listener, but he wouldn't speak during meetings. His boss told him he needed to start saying something.

When I probed Al about it, I asked him, "What was dinner time like for your family?" (One of the critical times when people learn their social skills.)

And Al said, "In my family, no one ever talked to each other while we were eating. Out of deference, it was always a very quiet time."

Dinner time for some families is a time for interchange, debate, talking about the day. For other families, though, it can be a very painful situation. So Al took his Family of Origin Dynamic into the workplace. When he was in a meeting he didn't say a word.

All of us bring that sense of family of origin dynamic into who we are as a leader and a contributor. And some of us were raised in a family where the rule was: "If you don't do this you're going to be punished."

How that comes out in organizations is in the form of: "It's my way or the highway."

That works both ways. Many times executives derail because that's their attitude towards their direct reports: "It's my way or the highway," which is a very arrogant statement. Also, when people give feedback sometimes and deal with consequences, they give it in a communication that says "my way or the highway."

Remember, what we learn in the family we bring into the workplace. This is potentially damaging because it's a threat, and people usually don't respond well to threats. Many employees will simply go along while they also go look for another job, or leave to start their own company.

So for Al, who had a lot of courage and a strong desire to make constant improvements in his life, I told him that next time he went into a meeting he should speak three times: once when the meeting opens, again towards the middle, and once more around the end. Especially towards the end because of the recency effect, that being what is said last people remember the most.

"Well, what do I say?" asked Al.

I told him he could (a) ask a question, (b) make a clarifying statement, or (c) add something to the conversation.

Sometimes all an employee like Al needs to do is ask a question. People in the meeting just need to hear their voice. So Al started doing that, and he started to get noticed a lot more. Al is extremely successful and is now seen as a potential successor after his boss retires. His boss has also put him out into a lot more presentations and professional meetings than he ever was before.

A Final Word About Feedback

According to a study of fifty-five large companies (95 percent with annual revenues of more than $1 billion), organizations that address derailment risks through the greater use of internal coaches report positive outcomes.

While almost all the companies use external coaches, especially for the C-level suite like CEO and CFO, about 60 percent are now using internal coaches. "External coaches often are used to 'save' an executive from failure when it's too late: like closing the barn door after the horse has already gone." (McDermott, Levinson and Newton: "What Coaching Can and Cannot Do for Your Organization," *Human Resource Planning*, June 2007).

The study went on to conclude that "using internal coaches in derailment cases, in contrast, may signal that the company takes performance issues seriously and is willing to invest the time of its own people, not just dollars, in supporting an employee's efforts to improve." Never sell yourself short as an internal coach, because you may be better positioned to leverage other company resources and people to help solve the issues that led to derailment.

6
Prescription Before Diagnosis Is Malpractice

First things first. Before you can help a derailed executive, you need to know why they jumped the track in the first place. Don't fall for that "no time or budget to assess the derailed executive" trap.

There is a saying in executive coaching that prescription before diagnosis is malpractice. In other words, it would be a breach of duty to treat the symptoms without doing tests to understand the root cause of the troubles.

Many a court of law has determined that <u>breach</u> of duty by a professional is negligence that has caused injury to a person. While it is highly unlikely you would be sued for lacking a systematic study of a failing executive's errors, the principle applies. Certainly skimpy assessments, or worst case, no diagnosis at all, is a breach of duty.

There has been a great deal of media coverage in the last few years about the subject of malpractice. A brief detour into this area of controversy further illustrates the point. The most publicized forms of malpractice are <u>medical malpractice</u> by physicians and <u>legal malpractice</u>

by attorneys, although malpractice suits against accountants (<u>Arthur Andersen</u>) and investment advisors (<u>Merrill Lynch</u>) have also been featured in the news.

By definition, malpractice is a type of negligence in which a <u>professional</u> fails to follow generally accepted professional standards. Let's consider this malpractice metaphor with a true tale from medicine.

A Crippling Illustration from the Medical World

How do medical practitioners diagnose patients? There are informal means, like interviews with patients about symptoms, and more formal means, such as lab tests. When you go to a physician with an ailment, for instance, you expect that they will run the appropriate tests and tell you the implications of the results. This might mean x-rays, blood tests, and urine and stool samples.

Here is an example of what a bad medical diagnosis can do. In 2008 the New York and New Jersey medical malpractice law firm of Gersowitz, Libo and Korek, P.C., won a $3.7 million settlement for Leopoldo Castillo against New York Presbyterian Hospital and Dr. Woosup Michael Park. During surgery, Castillo suffered spinal cord injury that made him paraplegic. The case was filed in the Supreme Court of the State of New York, County of New York.

On June 19, 2003, Leopoldo Castillo entered the emergency room at New York Presbyterian Hospital, complaining of pain in his lower and mid-back. Although he was originally diagnosed with pneumonia, his blood test results arrived the next day and showed an active staph infection. The hospital did not contact Castillo to tell him of the actual diagnosis.

Castillo's condition worsened, and he was admitted to New York Presbyterian Hospital on August 11th. He was then diagnosed with spinal osteomyelitis, an inflammation within his spinal column. Castillo was given intravenous antibiotics in the hospital and continued them at home, when he was released on August 27th.

Castillo's condition worsened still, and he was again admitted to New York Presbyterian Hospital on September 30th. An MRI of his spinal column showed further progression of the disease, and on October 2, 2003, Castillo underwent spinal decompression surgery.

During the surgery, Dr. Woosup Michael Park used Surgicel, a fabric to inhibit bleeding. However, Surgicel is not recommended for use in the spine. Less than three hours after his 3:15 a.m. surgery, Castillo reported he couldn't feel or move his legs. Nothing was done to identify the problem until late afternoon when a myelogram was performed at 4:30 p.m. Castillo was not operated upon until 6:15 p.m.

During this second surgery, physicians found the Surgicel had expanded and compressed Castillo's spinal cord, rendering him a paraplegic.

"Mr. Castillo's medical experience was a series of missteps, mistakes and missed opportunities," said Michael Fruhling, a GLK partner, "resulting in spinal cord injury, changing his life forever. New York Presbyterian Hospital and its doctors should be held accountable." The court agreed.

Implications for Coaching Derailed Executives

Now let's apply this to the world of coaching derailed executives.

Before embarking on turning around one of your derailing managers, you need to know what you are dealing with. Without a clear idea of the person's strengths and weaknesses, you are only guessing what is needed. This is no time to guess. Take the time to assess the true situation before you recommend a fix.

This is a lesson I learned from a derailed executive named John (real case, but not his real name). The telephone call from John's manager was intense and anxious. The manager described John's behavior as being hostile.

John would speak to people in critical ways. He would call people "stupid" and raise his voice when speaking with a peer on the phone in another part of the country. When I met John, he was somewhat distant, intense, and had that "big city" pushiness. John could not understand why he was being asked to work with a coach.

Furthermore, John could not understand why the others had so much of a problem with him. After a few coaching sessions, John seemed to become more positive. Suddenly, however, he refused to have me interview his peers. John could not handle the truth. He did not want to know what others really thought of him, and it was in fact difficult to make a diagnosis and develop a coaching plan.

His opposition regarding the 360-degree feedback assessment continued. This passive-aggressive style defended against truly making a diagnosis and engaging him to make meaningful change. Not only was John derailing, he made sure he derailed the coaching during the assessment phase.

Coaching Is Urgent; Assessment Is Important

In coaching a derailing manager, before you can prescribe exercises to change behaviors, you need to make a diagnosis identifying the nature or cause of the real malady. Here the term truly means "knowledge through and through." The more information you get the better.

But don't think that taking time to do the important work of assessing does not mean you are not doing the urgent work of coaching.

Even when you are making the assessment, you are beginning the coaching process. This is much like when you go to the doctor you feel better even before being prescribed a treatment. Why? Because you know you are doing something to solve the problem.

One part of the assessment is to determine if the person is actually coachable. That requires some coaching to begin with. So give them something to work on and see if you get some traction on positive change. This will provide another data point. Typically a lack of traction means the person may not want to change.

So how is your bedside manner? Like with a physician, one aspect of being a coach is to provide the results of the lab work (assessments) in a way that is motivating to the derailed executive. Giving feedback is both an art and a science. The art is that the style, tone, and personality of the words need to fit the personality of the person. If not, the information can be experienced as harsh and hurtful. Instead, you want to present the information in a way that will engage the person you are coaching.

Another aspect is that when the facts are stated in a way that is not acceptable, the derailed executive is apt to become defensive and has a greater chance of rationalizing the information away. When you give feedback, remember the derailed executive needs to feel supported and not attacked. This will also be important so the information will help the person see their behavior from a different perspective.

What is the Narcissistic Leader?

Not all derailments are the fault of the executive. An important part of the diagnosis is to determine if there is a narcissistic leader in the mix.

Bill (real story, not his real name) was a client who struggled with getting promoted. Bill was a very smart, highly analytical, and ambitious individual who did not take no for an answer. Yet Bill could be perceived as cold and distant because of his tendency to be more introverted than extroverted. Bill also came from a home where he was not acknowledged for speaking. In fact, in his home there was the rule of silence. The dictate when he was growing up was that "children are to be seen but not heard." Remarkably, Bill overcame his background and was able to move up as a financial person.

The real problem was Bill had a boss named Wendy who epitomized the narcissistic leader. These narcissistic leaders seek to be admired and aggressively pursue their goals. They are independent and aggressive and can be constantly looking for enemies and will, under extreme stress "degenerate into paranoia" (for a detailed look into this subject please see the article "Narcisstic Leaders-The Incredible Pros, The Inevitable Cons," by Michael Maccoby, *Harvard Business Review*, 1999).

Narcissistic leaders can have scores of followers and a great vision. On the flip side, they can also be sensitive to criticism and poor listeners and have a lack of empathy. They do not make good mentors.

Wendy only did what was in Wendy's best interest. In fact, Wendy spent a great deal of time coordinating meetings. She even coordinated a strategic planning meeting one month after the initial strategic planning meeting. She brought people from all over the world to attend. The result was that most people during the second meeting were bored and kept wondering why they were attending.

The answer was that Wendy needed an audience. As a true narcissist, Wendy needed attention. She craved the accolades and the reminders of what a wonderful boss and person she was. The result was her leadership capital and respect suffered. Yet, Wendy was adept and talented at managing up. She managed her "Executive Brand" with her superiors with aplomb and applause.

Bill came to realize that Wendy could get away with her behavior because of the superior numbers her business unit was generating (in business, exceeding one's financial goals can cover a multitude of sins).

Wendy had promised Bill a promotion. While Wendy did recommend Bill be promoted, because of a corporate snag with the final signature he did not get his promotion. His derailment was almost what would be considered "derailment by proxy." This means that the organization dynamics caused the derailment, not Bill's behavior.

Once this happened, Wendy was embarrassed. She then promised Bill to help him find another position. Instead of helping Bill, Wendy turned on him. One day Bill was seen as promotable, and the next day he was seen as a question mark when it came to his contribution to the organization.

Next Up, How to Use Assessments

There are three phases included in the assessment: fact finding, planning and consolidation, and implementation (these are discussed in detail in Chapter 7). This means that you must first have a way of gathering facts. Second, the planning and consolidation phase is putting the facts together and coming up with an initial set of themes and/or hypothesis about the coaching. Finally, the implementation phase is writing the coaching plan and the beginning of taking action. The person needs to start to take action on the coaching plan that is based on the facts from the assessment.

Each business goes through cycles. During each cycle a different kind and structure of management is needed. In the words of another author I recommend, Eric Flamholtz of UCLA, when an organization has not been fully successful in developing the internal systems it needs at a given stage of growth, it begins to experience "growing pains." For the past three decades Flamholtz has focused upon organizational growth and development, especially in entrepreneurial firms. Professor Flamholtz has authored several widely read books I recommend for all business coaches, including *Growing Pains: Transitioning from an Entrepreneurship to a Professionally Managed Firm*, and *Changing the Game: Managing Organizational Transformations of the First, Second, and Third Kinds*. His research has led to several frameworks that analyze the key building blocks of organizational success and the transitions from one stage of development to the next.

Obviously growing pains can cause derailments. What should you do if your diagnosis determines that the organization is going through growing pains? The main purpose of executive coaching is to help a particular style of manager be able to lead his or her team through the next life cycle of the business. As the coach or mentor, you need to help develop the executive so the derailment does not get worse and, in fact, assist the executive to be able to better lead the team into the next stage of corporate growth.

With all that in mind, let's proceed to the next chapter and examine how you do all this in the most effective way possible.

7
The Reinventor's Toolkit

Do you have a derailed executive that needs to make a comeback? Consider this inspiring story from the sport of football.

"Rarely did an athlete reach the highs and lows, and highs again, of Jim Plunkett," says Bob Carter of ESPN.

Plunkett, the youngest of three children, was raised by Mexican American parents who were both blind. Typhoid fever caused his mother, Carmen, to lose her sight since she was nineteen. His father, William, was legally blind but eked out a living as a news vendor.

Comeback #1: Plunkett's success as a California high school quarterback was followed by a shaky start in college, a beginning in which his coach almost made him quit quarterbacking and play defense. Then followed three remarkable seasons at Stanford, culminating with the 1970 Heisman Trophy, which made him the first Latino to win the annual award given to the best college player in the country.

Comeback #2: An outstanding rookie year in the NFL with the New England Patriots was followed by a string of injuries and, in the words of Carter, "adrift to the ranks of the ordinary." He even spent two years on the bench with the Raiders. And suddenly, from near-oblivion, a climb again to the peak as the 1981 Super Bowl Most Valuable Player.

"I'm proud of that game," Plunkett said of Oakland's 27–10 success over the Philadelphia Eagles. "Many people felt I was washed up, and I wasn't sure they were wrong."

Comeback #3: Age took its toll, and he was again benched in favor of younger quarterbacks. But three seasons later, Plunkett stepped back into the starter's role to lead the Raiders to another Super Bowl victory, this time over the Washington Redskins.

"He has to be one of the great comeback stories of our time," said Raiders owner Al Davis.

How to Plan an Executive Comeback

Is your company ready for a great comeback story? Then you as a manager are going to need to coach a comeback player of the year. In essence, you need to help them to reinvent their career. To do that, you need some specialized tools in your reinventor's toolkit.

When I advise the CEO of a company about a derailed executive, I warn him or her that comebacks don't happen overnight. But with persistent actions on the part of the manger/coach and the executive, it can happen. I have seen it time and again.

Meet Bill, Comeback Executive of the Year

Take Bill for example. Bill (real story, but not his real name) was president of a marketing entertainment business that is a subsidiary of an international company. The skills that enabled him to succeed early on in his career backfired on him, derailing him from his career track.

Bill was a driver. He was very achievement-driven and wanted the best for the company. He was willing to do whatever it would take for the team to be successful. Bill believed that the only thing in business is getting the job done. He believed that emotions do not belong in business and if someone can't get the job done they need to be replaced.

When I met Bill there were quite a few negative comments coming from his direct reports. His boss at the parent company was being briefed on a weekly basis on what a horrible leader he was, and there was starting to be some turnover. So the boss called me and said, "What can you do?"

So I went in to see his boss and went over the entire process as an overview with Bill. We found during an initial assessment stage that Bill had no idea what leadership was about. He thought that leadership was nothing but results, and his results were outstanding. So his belief system was that as long as he got the numbers to work, he was okay.

What Bill came to realize is that he could get better numbers, and he didn't have to be seen as a cold, distant, aggressive leader to do it. Truth was, Bill actually wanted to be seen as a personable, likable, engaging leader. He just never had a higher-up sit down with him and tell him how to do it. So Bill and I worked together for about six months and did a lot of work around him spending more time with each of his staff on a regular basis, asking about their career and really showing an ongoing interest in the welfare of each individual.

I shared with Bill a couple strategies for a comeback. One, you're going to have to act for a while. The second thing is that I started off small. In psychology there is a model for behavior change called Successive Approximation. What that means is that if you want to change your behavior, you break the larger behavior up into smaller segments. You get the person to have some successes in small ways so that when they get to the big ways they're feeling more comfortable.

So Bill and I started off about five minutes a day with just one of his direct reports, and that went well. So we added another one. Then we added team meetings, which he had never done. He learned how to make them more sociable, like by having food at the meeting. Bill did these steps on faith and then just started noticing that it was working. He was getting more positive feedback, and people were more productive.

Bill is a classic example of a derailed executive getting back on track with the help of a coach. He was such a great contributor, the management of his company just assumed he would make a great leader too. Wrong assumption. But with guidance, Bill made it back.

Begin with the Assessment Stage

Now let's apply this to your world. Managers need to know there are three stages to making a comeback. The first stage is the Assessment Stage, the second is the Ongoing Coaching Stage and the third is the Measurement Stage.

The goal of the Assessment Stage is to truly identify what the key behavioral issues are and to clarify the key motivations for change. A manager should want to target not only the key strengths of the derailed executive to leverage, but also two or three high-gain behaviors that, if the executive started to demonstrate, it would be considered evidence they were on the road to a comeback.

In the Assessment Stage there are three different tools involved.

1. The first tool is the manager must have a heart-to-heart talk with the executive. You want this to be a clear and honest, yet

supportive, feedback session with the individual. The feedback needs to be based on observable behavior. As a coach, you need to focus more on the behavior and not the personality. What you don't want the executive being coached to say is, "Wait a minute, I can't change my entire personality here." Remember, there is a business cost the organization is experiencing with the particular person's poor behavior. Part of that would be some information the CEO needs to get about the person that they are willing to talk about. What are their true career goals? Where are they going? Where do they want to get to in the next one to three years? If the person isn't opened up enough, how can they talk about any personal dynamics that are going on that are creating stress and problems?

2. The second tool of the Assessment Stage is some part of Self Assessment. It could be something as simple as a quick survey so the person can get an idea of how they perceive themselves. The basic prescription for wisdom from ancient Greek philosopher Socrates is to "know thyself" (the words that were carved over the entrance of the Oracle at Delphi). This is a simple instruction but an immensely difficult assignment. Socrates was a student of human nature, and his goal was to help all of us penetrate the greatest barriers to true knowledge: presumption and false belief. The next tool helps tackle those incorrect notions.

3. The third tool of the Assessment Stage is some type of 360-degree feedback survey. A 360-degree feedback is a methodology that provides each executive the opportunity to receive performance feedback from his or her supervisor and approximately six peers, reporting staff members, coworkers, and customers. The 360-process can be a series of interviews that the executive knows about so they can get some feedback. The critical piece is they

need to see how they are being perceived. The reason it's so critical is because if the executive needs to get on track and rebrand themselves, the coach and the executive need to know a baseline of how the executive is being perceived. Once all that information is collected, then the manager needs to give the feedback. Again, delivering that feedback is both a skill and an art. Together they go through what is learned about the individual, what their motivations are, and how they're being perceived. The goal is to percolate out one or two areas in which the executive will make developmental changes.

Stage Two Is Coaching

Right after these three tools are used the manager and derailed executive need to sit down and write out a plan of action. One aspect of that plan is that it needs to be as exact as possible, and it needs to include actions that the person can do.

So if the executive has burned a lot of bridges, then one series of steps would be to go and apologize. This may mean sitting down at a lunch with a group of peers or other team member and saying something like: "I'm really sorry. I know my behavior over the last six months has been less than stellar. I'm now aware of it, and I'd like to apologize. I will be working on it, and any feedback you can give me would be really helpful."

That's an action someone can do. It's very practical, it's to the point, and it gets at the issue. Sometimes it can be simple, like with one executive who was told he had to stop getting his e-mails on his Blackberry during meetings. He was informed that the message he was giving off was that whatever was going on in the meeting was not that important.

This is also an individual that scheduled a meeting with his international staff, and halfway through the meeting just up and left with no explanation. Everybody was saying "Where is he?" and nobody had realized he had basically put the phone down and never came back. Obviously, not an ideal leadership behavior.

Some executive coaches advocate a concept called 10-20-70. This method says that 10 percent of the development time needs to be in education, 20 percent needs to be more modeling, and the 70 percent is the trial and error learning. As a coach, you need to give executives some activity that they're going to get involved with that's going to help them change the behavior.

Overall, it is highly important that both the manager and the executive agree and commit to the plan that has been created in the Assessment Phase.

The Coaching Stage can also be broken down into three tools:

1. The first tool is for the manager to ask the executive, "What's new? What has changed since the last time you and I spoke?"
2. The second tool is to ask, "How are you doing on one section of the development plan that you and I have been talking about?" Let's say they tried to make amends and they apologized to someone in the company. What was the other person's reaction? Did they say, "Screw you! I'll never forgive you," or did the person say, "I really appreciate it. Here's what you can do for me"?
3. The third tool of the coaching phase is to determine the next step. "What are you going to do between now and the next time

I meet with you? And are you going to continue your reading? Are you going to experiment with delegating to somebody who says you never delegate to them? What is it you're going to commit to?"

In addition, the last step of every coaching session needs to be: When are we going to meet again? Never leave a coaching session without scheduling the next coaching session, because it's too easy to leave things open-ended. After each coaching session the manager might want to send a summary of all the items discussed and what the action items are.

Why follow up in writing? People forget about 80 percent of what is talked about within twenty-four hours, and it also gives an individual a customized, individualized manual to follow. That can be very, very helpful.

Stage Three Is Measurement

The manager should continue the coaching for as long as they can. Then the manager should periodically check in with the direct reports to find out how the individual is doing. Self-reporting is never as reliable as when other people do the reporting.

Sometime down the road, usually six months to a year, the manager will want to do the same 360-degree feedback on the executive. The second 360 is like going back to a doctor's office months after you've broken your leg and having the doctor take another x-ray to make sure it's healed.

Most times, after six months, you don't have the same individuals giving the same responses, but it's close enough to see if there's been any change. Then at the end of the feedback, the ending conversation is: What is the post-coaching plan? Are we going to see each other on a monthly basis? Are we going to continue bi-weekly meetings? Am I going to transfer you to someone else in the organization?

The other aspect of any type of comeback is that there is going to be one or two times where the individual is going to regress back to their old behavior. I'm currently working with an individual who has a tendency to scream and yell. He gets very frustrated if people aren't as intellectually quick as he is, and he shows his emotions by yelling. When an executive is under stress, they're going to have a tendency to go back to their old behavior. And that needs to be worked through.

So, managers, those are the tools and how to use them. The objective is to help the executive set a direction and stay the course. If you can keep someone in their job for an additional year without any negative consequences, then you've done quite well.

8
Should I Stay or Should I Go Now?

You can't save everybody. Nor should you. Many derailed executives are just daring you to fire them.

One day a CEO said to me, "I just can't get Byron to step it up."

Byron (real story, not his real name) was a director of engineering for a technology company. He was a long-term employee. The company, which started off as an entrepreneurial, family-based business that grew very fast, handled high amounts of high-tech manufacturing.

Now the production lines were getting stuck, the company wasn't getting product out the door fast enough, and they were having too many returns. Because Byron had been with the organization from day one, the CEO did not want to fire him.

"When you start off with a family-based business like ours," said the CEO, "there's a strong sense of loyalty."

A consultant was brought in to help with the engineering, and I was brought in to see if I could help Byron improve his leadership skills. The first couple sessions went well, and then all of a sudden Byron started changing his appointments. Following that he began to show total disinterest. So I told the CEO that I wasn't sure he was going to be engaged in the process. He might have a different agenda and it was getting in the way. Two weeks later the CEO called me to tell me that he was firing Byron.

What I told the CEO surprised him. "In a few months Byron will call you up and tell you that he's happier where he's at, and everyone will be able to move on." The CEO did hire a new director of engineering who was extremely sharp. Sure enough, Byron found a better job that was more in line with his skills. In truth, this worked out better for everyone.

The moral of the story is that sometimes it's better for everyone to move on.

When and How to Help Derailed Executives Out the Door

Up to this part of this book we have focused on the 80 percent that are able to get back on track after being derailed. However, there are 20 percent of derailed executives who, for a variety of reasons, fail to get enough traction to strike the balance between "too painful to keep" and "too valuable to get rid of."

Invariably, one of two scenarios transpires.

The first scenario goes something like this. During the assessment process the derailed executive realizes that part of the derailment was an unconscious wish to disengage from the company in the first place. So there's a voluntary departure where the individual says, "Because I couldn't pull the trigger myself and was unhappy, I was alienating others and decided it was time to leave."

This scenario plays out in many situations. Most decide not to go through the coaching process. As coach, if I detect it early on, I say to the executive, "You don't need me, you need a replacement consultant or you need a conversation with the CEO in order to work out a smooth transition that's in everybody's best interest. But to make yourself miserable and everybody else miserable really doesn't make much sense."

The second scenario is rare. This occurs with individuals who, for whatever reason, are recalcitrant to changing their behavior. Many of them are in complete denial and feel the problems are all about everybody else. These executives really are uncoachable. For me it is important to find this out as early as possible, because, as the coach, I'm not there to do outplacement to help people leave, I'm there to help them stay. Often times the company decides this person is causing too much pain, and the risk and investment in the coaching is too high. In this case, everybody would be better off if this person disengaged from the company.

I've only had two of these rare recalcitrant situations. In both instances I think the executive was still in the wrong job. The executive was truly unhappy and didn't see any value for making any substantive changes so they could get back on track. In one case the person rejected the coaching outright. He didn't want to do what it took to increase his ability. So the CEO called and said, "Time for him to leave," and I agreed.

(In other instances, the separation happens when I call back a year or two later at companies where the derailed executive had done well for a year. Many times the subsequent departure isn't even the executive's fault. In one case it was a year after the coaching. I was staying in touch with the client and I found out he was asked to leave, but so was everyone else on the executive staff because of a recent merger. However, five years later he was still telling me the coaching was valuable for him.)

I do whatever I can to coach somebody. These are last-ditch efforts to make the derailed executive aware that if they don't make these changes they may be in danger of losing their job. Happily, 80 percent make those changes.

Two Ways to Show Them the Door

There are two schools of thought when it comes to letting somebody go. One is to create transition time so the executive can find a new job. The other approach is that once the decision is made, do it as quickly as possible. My recommendation is to terminate the relationship in a speedy fashion. Once a decision has been made and the details (severance, etc.) have been worked out, make it happen now.

You hire slow, but you fire fast. The reason is when a person is kept in an organization when they know they're going to be leaving, there is the lame duck syndrome. These executives are rarely productive. Plus, if they've been derailing anyway and are negative or hostile, there's really no reason to believe they have any more value to the company. Keeping them around can create more problems than it's worth.

The message the senior leader making the decision should communicate is that the decision has been made. Once the person is gone everybody can breathe a big sigh of relief. Thankfully, it's time to move on.

Applying This to the Manager Coach

If you are the manager who is coaching the derailed executive, how do you know if this executive can get back on track? There are a several criteria.

The first criterion is whether they even want the coaching. If the executive doesn't want it, you shouldn't waste your time or your money. The second criterion is that within a short period of time, usually within four to six weeks, if you don't see any change then there's a probability this executive is not going to mentally engage in the coaching. The third criterion is if you ask the individual to go through the steps of the assessment or 360-degree feedback survey and you get constant pushback, then the person is not coachable at this time.

In today's world we live in a new corporate environment. The issue of loyalty always comes up, and I applaud the companies I work with because they cover all their bases to try and keep the individual within the organization.

There's been an evolution. From the 1940s to 1960s it was an implied cradle-to-grave contract. If you started working for IBM, then you ended your career with IBM.

Not any more. Because of this new reality, the loyalty issue becomes very confusing, even on the executive level. Many executives help companies get to a certain point and when they get to that point it's time to move on. There's more fluidity and mobility, and there just isn't the same loyalty aspect there used to be.

With layoffs and downsizing of organizations, the implicit contract has changed to become more of a free agency model. Individuals in this generation, having seen their parents being laid off, don't feel that same sense of loyalty. Companies know that when times are good they bring in lots of bodies, and when times aren't good there are layoffs or outsourcing to countries where the work is cheaper.

Just remember this: it's a business decision, not a personal decision.

9
Progress Is Our Most Important Product

Most executives do not want to be called average. For Luke it was a victory.

Luke (real story, not his real name) did an initial 360-degree feedback survey prior to my starting his coaching. His peer group rating was significantly low. In fact, the ratings were considered exceptionally below average on all dimensions.

After about eight months of coaching we conducted the same 360-degree feedback survey. Because Luke's ratings were so low, his scores weren't going to jump up too dramatically. Luke managed to go from below average up to average.

But when Luke looked at the 360-degree feedback results graphically it demonstrated that he had made considerable progress. When I showed the graph to the CEO, he was pleased because the 360-degree feedback survey substantiated his sense that things were getting better.

When I had the feedback session with Luke, he was happy that his hard work had paid off. So I always suggest to people that they do a pre-coaching and a post-coaching 360-degree feedback survey. The results of a pre and post coaching 360-degree feedback survey provides a type of objective measure of the behavioral changes the person accomplished during the coaching.

The results of the 360-degree feedback survey also provide suggestions for ongoing reinforcement of the changes. By continuing to use what he learned from the coaching and the feedback, Luke can now make the climb from ordinary to extraordinary.

How to Conduct "Back on Track" Benchmark Meetings

What is the return on investment—in time energy and money—of working with a derailed executive?

Of course, there are the subjective measures. One CEO told me, "We're not wondering what executive is going to show up: Dr. Jekyll or Mr. Hyde."

There are other comments I hear, such as: "Things just feel different" or "Well, there's less stress, less tension in the air. There's a sense of calmness."

Subjective measures are nice; however, there are objective measures that are critical. In business what gets measured gets managed. Or in the words of the English scientist Sir William Thompson, Lord Kelvin, who died in 1907: "When you can measure what you are speaking about, and express it in numbers, you know something about it; but when you cannot measure it, when you cannot express it in numbers, your knowledge of it is of a meager and unsatisfactory kind."

According to one author, while it is difficult to calculate the ROI of an investment in executive coaching, it is certainly not impossible.

"We can increase the chance of calculating a meaningful estimate of the bottom line impact of coaching if we carefully identify the highest priority objectives before the outset of the program," writes Tim Morin, the chief financial officer of WJM Associates (Morin, "Calculating ROI From executive Coaching," *WJM Management Advisor*, Sept. 08, 2004).

Morin contends the formula is straightforward:

$$\%ROI = \frac{\text{Benefits Achieved} - \text{Coaching Costs} \times 100}{\text{Coaching Costs}}$$

There are studies with solid numbers. According to the *Harvard Business Review*, three stock portfolios comprised only of companies that "spend aggressively on employment development" each outperformed the S&P 500 by 17–35 percent during 2003 (Bassi and McMurrer, "How's Your Return on People?", *Harvard Business Review*, March 2004). A study of senior-level executives at Fortune 1000 companies produced a 570% ROI on developmental coaching (McGovern et al, "Maximizing the Impact of Executive Coaching," *The Manchester Review*, 2001, Volume 6, Number 1).

The challenge is measuring the benefits achieved. There are tangible benefits to be considered, such as increased sales, decreased turnover, decreased absenteeism, and improved productivity. The intangible benefits can be reduced conflict, better teamwork, more productive meetings, and improved employee morale.

Three Success Metric Conversations

The final part of the process of helping a derailed executive to make a comeback is to hold regular benchmarking meetings. During these meetings the manager should give subjective and objective feedback to the executive.

When you tell derailed executives they're going to be measured through a process, then they are going to act more accountable. Never imply that the company is just going to put the executive through a coaching program, and if they get it great, and if they don't get it, that's okay too.

Measurement shows the seriousness with which the manager regards getting this derailed executive back on track. Here are three recommended measurement conversations to have during ongoing benchmarking meetings.

1. Time

Talk about time saved. One of the metrics of success that I ask the manager of a derailed executive about is, "How much time are you actually spending dealing with this problem?"

If the manager has done all the steps with the derailed executive, then they typically respond: "You know, now that you mention it, I'm actually spending a lot less time."

That is an important point of feedback for the manager to give the derailed executive who is making a comeback. In order for the executive to continue to make progress in their comeback, it is important to hear feedback about how much less time their manager is having to spend solving problems. This means the manager can spend more time on productive objectives like increasing revenues and decreasing expenses.

The feedback might sound something like this: "Since you've been on this track, what I've noticed that's been very helpful is that I've had more time to do the strategic aspects of being a CEO instead of spending time dealing with the negative behavior."

A manager's time has value, and at the minimum it is hourly rate of pay plus a multiplier for benefits and perks. Perhaps 1.5 x hourly rate would be a good place to start.

2. Web Survey

Talk about what others think. A second way to obtain an objective measure is to send out, on a monthly or quarterly basis, a very short survey to the respondent group around the derailing executive. You can use some of the Web-based tools, like Zoomerang, to do this easily and at low cost. Send out two or three questions that can be ranked from a negative three to a positive three. The negative three means the executive has gotten much worse, while a positive three means they've gotten much better. A zero means there has been no change.

The manager should tally those surveys up and present the findings at the ongoing benchmarking coaching sessions with the executive. The manager should give the executive the actual data to show them their behavior has changed and the perception of their behavior has changed. The way to give the feedback is very much like how you would give feedback to any employee. You might say something like, "I have a set of data, and I'd like to continually show you where you're making improvements and where you need additional energy." You can use that data as discussion points. Also, in conducting those meetings, it's important to ask the individual, if something has not improved significantly, what else do they need to do to make those improvements? What's working, what's not working?

3. 360-degree Feedback

Talk about what others say. The third objective measure would be to do a follow-up 360-degree feedback survey, usually around six months after the first 360 when the intervention coaching began. This before and after 360-degree feedback testing allows you to measure where the executive improved in their competencies. The manager can also see if there is a respondent group of employees that think the coached executive is doing better.

To illustrate, let's say it was the peer group that was having difficulty with the executive. Perhaps one of the job competencies the derailed executive was being coached on was to spend more time with subordinates. This measure can determine if that is happening.

According to the *Harvard Business Review*, executive coaches serve as suppliers of candor, "providing individual leaders with the objective feedback needed to nourish their growth" (Sherman and Freas, "The Wild West of Executive Coaching," *Harvard Business Review*, November 2004). "Well constructed 360s can identify particular behaviors with great precision and link them to corporate goals, values and leadership models."

Sherman and Freas go on to point out that by aggregating subjective judgments and making them anonymous, the 360-degree feedback surveys generate useful statistical data. Not all the judgments are fair; they do capture actual perceptions. For that reason, the insight that the 360s provide can be priceless.

A Closing Plea: Create a Culture That Prevents Derailment

When you conduct objective benchmark meetings, your company creates a culture that prevents executive derailment instead of trying to correct the derailment. I'm a firm believer that companies should have a 360 process on an annual basis for all of their managers and executives to make sure they know how they're doing. A 360-degree assessment is like going to your doctor for an annual checkup. The old adage is true that an ounce of prevention is worth a pound of cure.

If a manager can see that an executive is derailing and get help to them early, then there is a higher probability that the behavior can be corrected without significant damage to the organization, the culture, or the individual's executive's brand. Benchmarking with 360-degree management surveys and Web surveys is not that expensive to do. A company can begin with an outside source and after a while the managers can be trained to give the feedback.

Another pet peeve is that companies have a tendency to change their 360-degree feedback survey test on an ongoing basis. Typically a new HR person comes in, or the manager hears of a new 360 and changes it. I'm not a big believer in changing which test you use, but I am a big believer in finding one that really works for the company and using it at least two or three times. Every time you change the 360-degree feedback survey you're starting off with a new baseline. If the managers keep switching the survey tools, then the company won't be getting any longitudinal data.

10
Tracking Progress with Career GPS

How would you sail a boat from San Francisco to Honolulu? The answer may be more important than you think if you are coaching an executive.

Since my passion is deep-sea sport fishing, I have been amazed at the sensitivity and accuracy of tools like radar and Global Positioning Satellite (GPS) systems. I have been able to detect objects and boats and then navigate away. The radar also brings some semblance of security, since I can securely navigate through a fog with the help of my radar. If I get a little off course, the GPS instructs me how to get back on track.

In days of yore a mariner had little more than lighthouses to protect them from rocky shores and the sun and stars to guide them to reach their destination. To get from California to Hawaii, it would be helpful to have an idea of where you were going. In the words of the Roman statesman Seneca, "If one does not know what harbor one is making for, no wind is the right wind." You would also need navigational charts. This navigational aid would tell you the longitude and latitude of San Francisco and Honolulu. But what would keep you on course? Mariners would use a sextant to continually adjust their position.

Now let's fast forward to our day. With the advent of satellite technology, the GPS was developed. This technology uses the coordination and alignment of satellites to pinpoint your position anywhere in the world. The little device in your car or boat is "sensitive" to the satellite signals. Now drivers and ship captains can use the GPS to know where they are and to track a course.

If you have GPS in your car or boat, you know how great these devices can be. When you are off course, they do not shame you or blame you. If you miss a turn, they do not berate you. They just give you instructions on how to get back on course.

Guiding Mark to His Goal

Mark's goal was to be a leader of his company. This is the Honolulu he wanted to reach, but he kept getting off course. Like his own personal career GPS, I assisted him to find his way.

Mark (real story, not his real name) was a very bright, articulate, engaging, and ambitious senior leader. He was educated at one of the finest universities in engineering. He thought like an engineer and had a long, impressive resume with major international manufacturing companies. When I met Mark, I was called in to provide coaching to upgrade his skills so he could be part of the leadership of the company.

After a 360-degree feedback survey, the message back from his direct reports was that he did not show enough strength as a leader. He was not decisive enough to make tough decisions. Therefore, he allowed too many people issues to slide by. The result was resentment. Since he was trained as an engineer, he had not taken the time to develop his emotional intelligence.

Now Mark could have given up and just accepted a technical role in the organization.

During our coaching, I suggested to him that being stronger was part of being an effective leader. Showing strength was going to be critical. Since he truly wanted to be a leader, he took risks. As we worked together I kept giving him signals if he was on course or off course. There was one situation where he actually stopped an interview because he felt it was a waste of time for everyone. He stopped the interview with professionalism, but the message to his team was that he was strong enough. His leadership capital increased exponentially.

All Executives Need Career GPS

Executives need a special kind of GPS. They need coaches who keep telling them if they are on the right course or straying off the mark.

The metaphor for the radar and leadership is quite simple. Leaders and employees alike send and receive subtle emotional "beams" that will be received either as positive or negative. This final chapter looks at how you can coach both derailing and on-track executives to be aware of the emotions that are sent out and their possible impact. Understanding the power of these emotional and psychological "beams" is critical in helping anyone become a more effective leader.

Surely the best possible outcome when it comes to executive derailment is to prevent it in the first place. When selecting executives, the objective should be to hire slow and fire fast. There is an old adage that you can "solve the problem before it walks in the door, or after." But most leaders find selection a true challenge because people change. Even though people are good at interviewing, that does not necessarily mean they will be good employees. Also, hiring for fit is critically important.

Not only do people need to have the necessary skills, but their character needs to fit into the culture.

Setting Executives Up to Fail

A cousin of the Peter Principle (promoting people to their level of incompetence, which was discussed in Chapter 3) is the Setting Up to Fail Syndrome. This means that when a company makes a decision to promote they usually do not provide the necessary training and or coaching. Instead of being set up to succeed, these executives are set up to fail. This truly puts an executive in danger of derailing, for one of the reasons people derail is that they no longer fit into their position because they reached either their Peter Principle or are in the throes of being set up to fail.

Steve (real story, not his real name) was a senior executive at an international consulting firm. He had a pedigree of degrees from the best universities in the nation. He was articulate, forceful, convincing, and engaging. When I began to coach him, he talked about being asked to leave the company in an interesting way. With Steve, there was no hint in his voice of resentment.

The absence of resentment was the clue. When asked about his journey of departure, Steve said that looking back he "set up" the situation so he would derail. He resisted the new leadership, expressed his displeasure constantly, and became a royal pain in the rear end. He further acknowledged that he set the derailment up because he was unhappy and "could not pull the trigger on himself." His derailment was his escape hatch, his exodus strategy from a miserable work situation.

The lesson for coaches is that you need to be sensitive to the messages your derailed executive may be giving you. Like Steve, you need to see what messages are being sent back to you. You need to ask yourself, is this person happy in their position? Have they outgrown the company or the function?

The next question, once you have the conversation, is to discuss if this person would in fact be happier at another company. Instead of creating a situation where both of you are frustrated, find a humane but quick plan for a departure.

If the person is worth keeping, coach the person to list their likes and dislikes of the position. Discuss the gaps. Then determine what can be done so they will become happier and therefore get back on track. But remember: the person needs to be clear that their current behavior is not acceptable. They need to understand the health of the organization takes precedence over their career happiness.

Why Highly Technical Professionals Derail

One of my interests is working with scientists and people who have advanced degrees with a strong analytical bent (possibly because of my own background). One reason why I like coaching these technical executives is that these individuals make such a meaningful contribution. The common reality is that these individuals who are technical professionals are promoted because they were so good at what they did. One of my missions is to help them transition from being a technical professional to a leader.

Many of them go into the sciences because they want to build things, not work with people. Management was probably something they did not study in college or grad school. For instance, there was Bill (real story, not his real name). Bill was a senior scientist who went through a coaching program after it was discovered he did not have a calling for managing people. His request was to return to be a senior scientist and not continue to pursue a role of manager.

Bill ended up being very successful as a scientist, and his experiment with managing people was a good experience. He now had clarity about his true career calling, and that management was surely not for him. His curiosity had been satisfied. Bill learned his course as a scientist was his calling, and he could focus on being the best scientist possible.

The moral of the story is: technical competence does not always yield managerial competence.

All companies hunger for superstar employees. The hunger for superstar employees leads to promoting them into managers. Companies also hunger for superstar managers and leaders. In order to help a superstar successfully transition from employee to manager without derailing, they need to be coached.

But be careful. Many times superstars have a strong ego and are not aware of their need for help. So, one convincing strategy is to tell them the best get better by ongoing coaching and development. You need to sell them on the idea that to truly be set up to succeed they could benefit from coaching.

A Few Closing Thoughts

While this book will help improve your ability to effectively coach derailed executives and manage your termination process if necessary, the information here is of a general nature and not intended as legal advice nor a substitute for getting specific legal advice on your particular situation.

Of course, nobody likes to terminate an executive. So here are my three tips for avoiding the problem.

Tip #1: Hire Great in the First Place. By screening potential employees for past behaviors and attitudes, you can dramatically reduce the costs of hiring bad people, and make your workplace more productive, happier, safer, and more profitable. Combine an efficient prescreening assessment with an effective pre-employment background check, and you can cut your risk by half or more.

Tip #2: Hire and Promote for Job Fit. A well-documented study, published in *Harvard Business Review* concludes that "Job Match" is by far the most reliable predictor of effectiveness on the job (Greenberg and Greenberg, "Job Matching for Better Sales Performance." *Harvard Business Review*, Volume 58, No. 5, Sept 1, 1980). The study considered many factors including the age, sex, race, education, and experience of approximately 300,000 subjects. It evaluated their job performance and found no significant statistical differences, except in the area of "Job Match." The conclusion was this: "It's not experience that counts or college degrees or other accepted factors; success hinges on a fit with the job."

If success is determined by job fit, your challenge is to predict that fit. This requires that you measure thinking style, behavioral traits, and occupational interests, and that you do so in a cost-effective way. Assessments are an efficient way to predict job fit. With an assessment, an employer can assure that the people hired fit their new jobs; that the people promoted can succeed in the new position; that employees can identify a career path likely to work; and that newly opened jobs can be filled from within, with a high probability of success.

Tip #3: Improve Managers and Keep Your Best People. People quit people; they don't quit jobs. Guess which people they are most likely to quit? Hint: Managers have the most significant impact on a worker's daily activities, the mood of the work setting, and the reward structure on the job.

Identifying the strengths and weaknesses of your managers, and improving their most critical skills, is a key component of keeping your best people. In this economy, budgets for training have been curtailed, making it difficult to find the money to improve management skills. Many companies are concerned about wasting money on training employees that will leave. As author, salesperson, and speaker Zig Ziglar said, though, "If you think it's expensive to train people and lose them, try not training them and keeping them!"

Best wishes with coaching the derailed executives in your business. Unfortunately there will always be know-it-alls, bullies, prima donnas, and passive aggressors. But don't tolerate them for one day. If they were exceptional once, then coach these prodigal executives to return to greatness. My bias is to bring in an outside coach (hey, it's what I love to do); but if you can't, then coach this person yourself. Assess the situation so they get honest feedback. Commit to coaching on a regular basis. Ignore the nagging doubts that these derailed executives can't be trained because people don't change. That is a common misconception.

The prodigal executive can come home. You can coach them to return. I wish you success in making that happen.

About the Author

Bruce A. Heller, Ph.D., has more than twenty years experience consulting with leaders of Fortune 500 companies, growing businesses, and start-ups. He is an expert in the areas of leadership development, coaching derailing executives, and executive assessment. Dr. Heller brings a wealth of business experience and training as a psychologist to each client engagement.

His strengths lie in improving productivity and performance through comprehensive assessment, facilitation, coaching, and training. Dr. Heller has taught graduate classes on the psychology of individual and group development at Loyola Marymount, Antioch, and Pepperdine University. He has been a guest lecturer at UCLA, UC Riverside, and Vistage (Formerly TEC). Bruce holds a Ph.D. and a Master's Degree in Education from the University of Southern California. He has a Bachelor of Arts Degree from San Diego State University, where he graduated Phil Beta Kappa and was honored a National Science Foundation Undergraduate Research Grant.

You can reach him at:

The Heller Group, Inc.
16830 Ventura Blvd.
Suite 415
Encino, CA 91436

Phone: 818-981-4310
Fax: 818-501-3707
Email:BruceHeller@hellergroupinc.com
www.hellergroupinc.com

CPSIA information can be obtained at www.ICGtesting.com
Printed in the USA
LVOW13s2340241013
358296LV00001B/76/P